MAN POWER

HOW TO WIN THE
WOMAN YOU WANT

MAN POWER

HOW TO WIN THE WOMAN YOU WANT

TRACY CABOT

St. Martin's Press   New York

Design by Karin Batten

Library of Congress Cataloging-in-Publication Data

Cabot, Tracy.
    Man power : how to win the woman you want
    / by Tracy Cabot.
        p. cm.
    ISBN 0-312-01787-1 : $16.95
    1. Love.   2. Mate selection.   3. Interpersonal relations.
I. Title.
HQ801.C253 1988
646.7'7--dc19   87-36692
                                                            CIP

First Edition

10 9 8 7 6 5 4 3 2 1

To my husband, Marshall,
and all men who love women

ACKNOWLEDGMENTS

My husband, Marshall, for his loving support and unerring "male viewpoint."

My editor, Toni Lopopolo, for being first to realize male-bashing was out and loving men was in.

My agent, Robert Gottlieb, for his constant encouragement and astute guidance.

CONTENTS

A PERSONAL NOTE FROM THE AUTHOR

My life was a series of relationships that either fizzled out or ended in disaster, and I had a better chance of being killed by a terrorist than of being married until I discovered a method for creating the chemistry of love. I used it in my own life and it worked like magic. I have been happily married now for several years. My friends used the techniques and they were successful. I wrote about our success in *How to Make a Man Fall in Love With You,* and thousands of women used my methods to make the man they wanted fall in love with them.

When I first suggested writing about these powerful techniques in a book for men, many women expressed doubt. "Don't men have power enough? We're the ones who need help. Why not keep the information private, just for us? Besides, men don't care about love."

How to Make a Man Fall in Love With You was written just for women because I was going along on the assumption that men just wanted to know "how to score" or "how to pick up girls." But as I traveled in the United States and Europe, appearing on talk shows and conducting seminars, I noticed that many, many men definitely do care about love.

Often a male cameraman or technician would come up to me after a show with a question about his love relationship. As many men as women were showing up at bookstore autograph parties with relationship problems they wanted to solve. My seminars and workshops were attracting equal numbers of men and women, and my private practice was divided almost evenly between the sexes. Men began to complain to me that nobody was writing books for them about how to win at love. So they bought *How to Make a Man Fall in Love With You* and tried to reverse the techniques, often on the recommendation of their psychologists or therapists.

Men do care about love, and there are more good men than the recent rash of man-bashing books would indicate. There are nice men, men worthy and deserving of love. Men who love women. This book is for them.

In a world of searching and insecurity, of singles' bars and mid-life crises, dating services and therapy groups, there is a desperate shortage of mature, mutual love. Millions of men, ready for a loving, committed relationship, have been unable to find the love they want.

Man Power: How to Win the Woman You Want is for every man who isn't getting the kind of love he wants right now. If you follow the Man Power Method exactly, I guarantee that you too will be able to win the woman you really want.

INTRODUCTION

People who are in love communicate on a deeper level than other people. Lovers seem to read each other's minds intuitively. They are in tune with each other in a special way. They have reached into each other's inner beings. You know immediately when you see them that they belong together. They have the magic.

Now, for the first time, you can create the magic of love whenever you want. You don't have to wait for the chemistry to happen by accident. You can take charge of your personal life and get it under control once and for all.

If you've ever wondered, "Why can't she appreciate me? Can't she see how much I love her?" and if love seems to be passing you by, you can learn to turn disinterest into interest, indifference into caring, and friendship into love by using the Man Power Method.

Modern psychology tells us that each of us is dominated by what he or she sees, hears, or feels. By learning to discern whether your woman is influenced primarily by what she sees, hears, or feels, you will understand how to make her feel love. You'll know exactly the right words to say, and precisely the right moves to make, to create the intimacy and trust that form the basis of a lasting love relationship.

She will be irresistibly drawn to you. Her attention will be riveted on you. She'll feel that you are her true soul mate, that you alone understand her. You'll know exactly how to please her. Your timing will be faultless. You'll never hear the words "No thanks" again, because you'll know how to get her to say yes to whatever you want. By following the Man Power Method, you will be able to make the woman you want yours forever.

MAN POWER

HOW TO WIN THE WOMAN YOU WANT

Witches, Bitches, and Crazy Ladies

Some women just don't deserve your love. They are the crazy-makers—the women who tap dance on your brain and drain your psyche. By learning the Man Power Method for getting power over women, you will be able to pick and choose, bypassing the women who hurt and finding the ones who want to love. You'll learn how to have a meaningful, lasting, and fulfilling life with the woman of your choice and how to control a relationship so that it doesn't end in disaster.

If your relationships never seem to bring you anything but pain, if "the fucking you get isn't worth the fucking you get," if you feel that all women are bitches, it's time to figure out why you're winding up with the bitch brigade. You may have a fatal fascination for the wrong kind of femme fatale.

Just because you've been involved in go-nowhere, crazy-love relationships with women who've treated you badly doesn't mean you are incapable of sane love. It may simply mean you're choosing witches, bitches, and crazy ladies, and there are a lot of them out there.

1

Why Nice Men Wind Up With Witches, Bitches, and Crazy Ladies

I've found that there are five major reasons why perfectly nice men wind up with perfectly rotten women.

1. It takes a very nice man to put up with some of these women. Witches, bitches, and crazy ladies aren't dumb. They always pick nice men, men who won't leave at the first sign of craziness, men who want to help, men who will wait for sanity to return.
2. By picking women who treat them badly, some men are able to avoid a committed relationship. The worse she acts, the more justified the man is in avoiding commitment. Sometimes a man even drives a woman to act crazy and then says, "See, I knew I shouldn't get too involved."
3. Often a nice man will find a perfectly nice woman and, by letting her get away with bad behavior, will accidentally teach her how to act like a bitch and walk all over him, never realizing what he's doing.
4. Sometimes a man needs the excitement a truly crazy lady brings to his life. At any minute she may attempt suicide, crash the car, burn the house, leave, or have a disastrous affair. What thrill can compete with the living soap opera a truly crazy lady brings to his dreary everyday life?
5. There are other "advantages" to having a crazy lady in your life. If you're the type who needs to take care of someone, you have a built-in outlet for your caretaking instincts. If you're insecure and have low self-esteem, you always have someone to whom you feel superior. If you need a victim, someone to abuse, either physically or verbally, she'll probably fill the bill. You can torment her as if you were a little boy pulling a little girl's pigtail, and she won't leave— she'll just get crazier.

Why Not Go Along for the Ride?

Why not pick a crazy lady if she fulfills your needs? Because those are not healthy needs. In a crazy-lady relationship, you both lose. She just gets crazier and so do you. Then you're stuck. You're afraid of what she might do if you leave, but if you stay, your life will never be sane.

Leaving a witch, bitch, or crazy lady is tough because she's sexy and intriguing. That's how she gets away with her outrageous behavior. She is so good-looking, or so good in bed, that men overlook her insanity. Often she's not intentionally bitchy or even conscious of it. She's just been spoiled, by men and by women, ever since she was the "prettiest little girl at the party."

Have you ever fallen for a beautiful girl and let her get away with murder? Of course you have, and in so doing you've made her even more spoiled, and bitchier, for the next guy.

Witches, bitches, and crazy ladies are difficult, inconsiderate, and selfish, but they aren't walking around with signs on their heads that say, "I'm a bitch," "I'm a witch," or "I'm a crazy lady." Being able to spot them ahead of time can be tricky. If you meet any of these classics, move on.

Twelve Classic Bitches, Witches, and Crazy Ladies to Avoid at All Costs

1. THE DEVIANT

At first, the Deviant is a lot of fun, the bad little girl down the block your mother always told you to stay away from. In the beginning, you think it's a kick to be with her. She's always doing the unexpected. If the light says red, she zooms through. If the sign says don't smoke in the airplane john, she lights up a joint. If there's a new illegal drug, she's the first to try it. If there's a new illicit or amoral activity, she gets excited and can't wait to do it.

The Deviant is irresistible in bed, where her deviant behavior really shines. No matter what sex act you've imagined, she'll be willing to try it. If you haven't even thought of it, she'll bring it up. Her imagination is endless. That's why you find it so hard to leave her, even after you've bailed her out of jail a few times on assorted charges and she's almost gotten you arrested too. Deep in your heart, you know there will never be sex like this again. You know your deviant woman is a once-in-a-life-time opportunity to experience true decadence.

The biggest problem with the Deviant is that she gets you into trouble. Trouble with the police, the DMV, the IRS, your parents, your boss, your landlord, your friends, and anyone else who is a regular member of straight society.

Besides, no matter how much fun she seems to be having with you, the Deviant is really just a thrill whore— she'll suck you off in the front seat of a Ferrari Daytona at 180 miles per hour, but if some guy offers to fuck her while skydiving, she'll be gone in a flash.

2. THE ACHIEVER

The Achiever already makes more money than you do, and she likes it that way. It gives her power she's too insecure to live without.

On the surface, the Achiever may look like the dream woman of the 1980s. She's bright, witty, and attractive. If you're the kind of guy who's not put off by high-powered women, you find it flattering that she's chosen you over all the high-powered guys she meets at work.

In the beginning, your romance with the Achiever is a

rush. You enjoy the fast pace, the time-is-more-important-than-money lifestyle. You even have occasional fantasies of being a kept man, of living a life of leisure on her fantastic salary.

Then her secretary calls to tell you that she's off to the airport for an out-of-town meeting and can't make the trip to Hawaii you'd been planning for six months. Or she proposes going into business together. She's got it all figured out, and she can raise the money. Soon after that, your ulcers start. If the business is a failure, your relationship falls apart. More likely, the business will be a roaring success, and you'll never see her without making an appointment with her administrative assistant.

Life with the Achiever means you come after the achievement. Whatever is going on in your relationship is trivial compared with her next presentation, merger, sale, or promotion. And you can forget a homelife. For her, quality time together is a round of golf shared with some visiting businessmen. She won't have sex unless she can reach the bedside phone, in case there's a business call.

The Achiever is hell to live with, but you won't get sympathy from anyone. She'll claim she's doing it all "for us." Your parents will be in awe of her and think you're a complainer, and your male friends will say you got just what you deserve.

With the Achiever, you may be lonely, but you'll never starve.

3. LOLITA

Lolita is so adorable, so affectionate, so malleable, so sexy, and so young. She looks up to you as the wise teacher and you love the role. You imagine yourself molding her into the grown-up woman of your dreams. You'll just keep her around until she's matured into your own little Stepford

Wife, showing her the ropes, keeping her pure and shel-
tered. If you really believe that, you need your head ex-
amined.

Actually, she's just discovered her sexual power and is
trying it out on you. She's also probable jailbait, but you
don't care. You're flattered at your ability to attract a
much younger woman and couldn't care less what anyone
says.

What she really wants is to get even with Daddy by
screwing you, and as soon as some twenty-year-old Adonis
shows up, she'll leave you and shower him with all the
wonderful pleasures you've taught her how to provide.
Inexperienced lout that he is, he won't appreciate her,
which will only make her love him more.

She'll possibly be ready for a serious relationship in
about fifteen years, but by that time you'll be too old to
enjoy her.

4. THE TIME BOMB

The Time Bomb is an emotionally lethal weapon that goes
off with no warning just when you think your lives have
finally settled down.

The most frightening thing about the Time Bomb is
that she looks so normal on the surface; you can't tell she's
a Time Bomb until she explodes on you a couple of times.
She's the type who waits to yell "I don't" in the middle of
your wedding ceremony. Or she has an affair with your
best friend and gets pregnant, and you don't know whose
kid it is. Or she just disappears one day, leaving you with
two-year-old Junior.

There are some clues, but she's so cute and seems so
perfect that you choose to overlook them. The most obvious clue is that if she's so great-looking, such perfect wife
material, why hasn't someone snatched her up and kept
her? How come she's running loose?

Another clue to a Time Bomb–type personality is that she seems to have no friends she's known for a long time. Her parents have given up on her. That's because she's done her exploding number on them so many times. Usually she doesn't live too close to home, because she needs new territory, some place where people don't know her yet. Time Bombs always seem too good to be true—and they are.

You can never relax with a Time Bomb because you know the explosion will eventually take place. When she does blow up and leave you, though, you'll do almost anything to get her back, because she's so sweet to be around between uproars. No matter how many times she promises to behave, don't believe her. You can be sure another blowup is brewing. It's just a matter of time.

5. THE TRUE BELIEVER

The True Believer is always on the cutting edge of whatever new philosophy, psychology, or new-wave anything comes along. She has (or may even be) a channeler, an astrologer, a fortune-teller, a healer, a yogi, a spiritual master—and a true answer to all the world's problems. She also has a crystal (or even a whole roomful), a Ouija board, a t'ai chi class, yoga and meditation tapes, healing music, tarot cards, and I Ching coins. She is open to anything, including you, as long as you believe.

So you follow her out into the desert in the middle of the night to wait for spaceship Moonbeam to land and take you off into the next world, and so what if it doesn't come? You've done a lot more for women and had a lot less fun.

One man I know gave up a thriving law practice to follow a True Believer on a trek across India. They were both to have come back as gods. What happened is they broke up. Walking across India can get on your nerves if

you don't believe enough. Another man and his beloved
went to a "firewalk," where they both walked barefoot
across a twelve-foot bed of red-hot coals. "So I got a couple
blisters," he joked afterward. "At least I proved you don't
have to be a total believer not to burn to a crisp." I am
always amazed how men will follow a True Believer.

The True Believer does have some advantages, though.
She doesn't eat meat and she doesn't drink, so she's a
cheap date. She comes with a built-in group of friends and
preset rules. You never have to make any decisions, you
just have to follow along with the group, and believe,
believe, believe. Of course, once an ugly doubt has raised
its head, the romance is over.

6. THE MAN HATER

Accept it. Some women just don't like men, often with
good cause. The Man Hater loves to find a nice guy like
you who'll stand there while she takes out her hostility for
what other men have done to her. You'll wind up paying
for the transgressions of everyone from the boy who tor-
mented her in kindergarten to her younger brother, her
father, her uncle Harry, and even her first husband.

Man Haters look like ordinary women when you meet
them, but there are signs of incipient man-hating. Man
Haters consistently put down men and praise women. In
the beginning, the Man Hater pretends that you're different from all those other men who've treated her badly,
but soon she begins to see signs that you're really not. By
this time, you're in love with her, so you try to convince
her by the power of your love that you're one of the good
guys.

The trouble with a Man Hater is that she doesn't recognize a good guy when she gets one. Even the smallest
indiscretion, like leaving the toilet seat up or not being
able to find something when it's right under your nose,

will reveal the permanent unforgivable rotten core she sees lurking inside all men.

The Man Hater often covers her basic dislike and mistrust of all men with feminist grievances. She's not putting down men, she's defending women.

No matter how much you love a Man Hater, you won't be able to make up for the wrongs suffered by her and all the other women in the world, which she'll expect you to do. Don't even *think* about being the good guy who changes her mind about men.

7. THE WAFFLER

The Waffler just can't make up her mind. She can't decide if she wants you or someone else. She can't decide if she wants to have a relationship or just fool around. One week she's a member of the girls-just-want-have-fun club, and the next she's talking about having babies.

The Waffler hates making dates in advance. "Call me Friday and we'll talk about Saturday night." Or "I won't know until I talk to my veterinarian to see how my sick cat is doing." Greed keeps the Waffler from making any irrevocable decisions. If she commits to going out with you too soon, well, something better may just come along and then where will she be?

The Waffler breaks dates all the time, because something better does come along or because she simply changes her mind. The Waffler has a fantasy man in mind and a fantasy relationship. Since nobody's reality ever lives up to her fantasies, a Waffler who makes a date ahead of time begins to dread the date as it approaches. She knows you can never be as terrific as she is hoping you'll be.

One reason the Waffler isn't fun to be with is because she's always yearning for someone else, someone taller, stronger, richer, better in bed—someone she will never find. The good part is that the Waffler's constant search for something better means she never stays with anyone too long.

8. THE VIRGIN

—or almost. The Virgin has never had an orgasm before, and may never again without your constant attention. And there are guilt trips to come. If you introduce her to a sport and she hurts herself, it's your fault. If you take her out to eat and she gets food poisoning, it's your fault. And of course, if the relationship doesn't work out, it's definitely your fault, since she was a virgin, or almost, before she got involved with you.

Fooling around with the Virgin is fun for a while, but it's like the electric company. Once you turn on the juice, you have to keep paying the bills. And paying and paying. Most Virgins have never heard of birth control, and often don't believe in it if they have heard of it. So they often get pregnant, and they definitely don't believe in abortion. So you're stuck, for life. With the Virgin, the Virgin's parents, church choir, and a very conservative lifestyle.

The Virgin loves you as long as everything you do would be approved by the Supreme Court or the parish priest. It's an ego trip to think that you're the guy who finally broke through her reserve, that only you can make Ms. Frigid act like a sexual lunatic in bed. But the ego massage lasts only so long, and then you realize that making her come isn't worth the hassle.

9. THE WALKING WOUNDED

Because she is just divorced or ending a long-term relationship, the Walking Wounded needs a transitional relationship while she figures out what happened, who she is, where her self-esteem went, and what she's going to do with her life.

Should you make the mistake of accepting the assignment, you will be in for an unlimited amount of crying towel duty. The Walking Wounded will spend hours telling you how that monster did her wrong. She'll replay her last relationship ad nauseum, and your life will be filled with stories of what he did yesterday and today and what he's going to do tomorrow.

She spends most of her time talking, thinking, wondering, worrying about him instead of you. You will always feel as if she loves him more than she loves you, even though he's treated her so badly; and so you try harder to treat her even better. You bring flowers, you tell her you love her forty times a day, you buy her presents. But no matter what you do, the shadow of her broken heart hangs over your relationship.

She's just not ready for prime-time relating until she stops talking about him all the time, stops worrying about what she did or didn't get in the divorce, quits wondering what he does or doesn't do, and makes you her prime concern.

10. THE SUPERVISOR

The Supervisor is a perfectionist who goes around assessing the performance of the world to see if it lives up to her exalted standards. Since nothing is ever perfect, she's constantly telling you what's wrong with everything.

At first, it's fun. You're flattered that someone with such high expectations and good taste has chosen you. So it's you and she, the two perfect people, lined up against an imperfect world. But soon you start to realize the imperfections in each other, and you turn on each other.

She realizes that your lapels are three-eighths of an inch too wide and that you're wearing last year's cuff. No sooner does she get all your clothes updated than she realizes that something is wrong with your job, or your car, or your apartment. Finding things wrong with the world is her way of life, so she can be very difficult to live with on an everyday basis.

You begin to realize that no matter what you do, no matter how much you let her run your life, it's still not perfect enough. When she realizes that you can't do anything right, she takes over living for you. Eventually, either you succumb, have a frontal lobotomy, and spend the rest of your life following her around; or you grow a beard and start wearing clothes from the Salvation Army to get her out of your life.

11. THE STARLET

Breathlessly gorgeous, the Starlet is the ultimate arm-piece at a cocktail party. Once you start a conversation with her, though, the image is shattered. There's nothing more disconcerting than finding out that the woman of your dreams wants to be a *Playboy* centerfold—"Seriously, sure! I mean, you know, just to get my career started!"

You'll probably have her for about two dates if you promise to introduce her to your brother-in-law at the William Morris Agency. She's always looking for bigger game, though, so keep an eye on her. Kissinger was right—"Power is an aphrodisiac." Let her meet an actor, ex-astronaut, or even a newsworthy politician, and she's gone for the night. She'll be back in the morning, though.

Men who marry starlets often wind up in the divorce courts because very few starlets get to be stars. When they don't, they invariably blame the men in their lives and either make them miserable or dump them.

One Starlet per customer is excusable, but if you get hooked on them, you're dippier than they are.

12. THE CRAZY LADY

There are lots of crazy ladies. Trying to avoid them is very tricky because craziness can be charming, enchanting, and bewitching, and also because there are so many degrees of craziness. Contrary to popular belief, the craziest ladies have not been in therapy.

The ones who are truly crazy stay far, far away from help. But there are signs that a woman is too disturbed for you to have a serious relationship with her. Addiction, constant depression, uncontrollable hostility, the hearing of voices, and an inability to be happy are all signs of a crazy lady.

Never try to save a crazy lady. Actually, saving anyone is impossible anyway. People have to save themselves. If you find a woman who needs years of therapy to get better, don't think you can save her by sending her to the therapist. What usually happens when people get better is that they change. So she gets better, changes, and doesn't want you anymore. Saving crazies is a no-win situation.

Bitch Avoidance

Bitches know intuitively when they have you hooked. Just as soon as you say "I love you" or call one time too often, they start tap dancing on your brain and trying to get you to jump through hoops. Like a cleverly adjusted gambling machine in Las Vegas, they know how to give back just enough to keep you hooked and yet they never give you enough to keep you happy.

Getting out of a relationship, once you're hooked, is a lot harder than avoiding it in the first place. The best way to avoid witches, bitches, and crazy ladies of all varieties is to understand that they have neurotic *needs,* whereas normal women have normal *wants.*

What Normal Women Want

Marriage
Children
Girlfriends
Family ties
Laughs
Sympathy
Romance
Shopping
Presents
Attention
Affection
Kindness
Sex
Agreement

What Witches, Bitches, and Crazy Ladies Need

To use you for their own agenda without caring what happens to you
A man to make their lives okay
Everything all at once
Unconditional love
An endless party

If you're attracted to a woman who looks like one of the classic witches, bitches, or crazy ladies, or if she seems to have a neurotic need, stay away. If she's really sexy and coming on to you, it's hard to stay away, but you can reprogram that first reaction. Instead of thinking, "I wonder what she'd be like in bed," try thinking, "Whoops, there goes trouble for somebody, but it isn't going to be me!"

Remember, there's nothing wrong with falling in love with a normal, well-adjusted woman.

First Aid for Chronic Sufferers From Witches, Bitches, and Crazy Ladies

1. Start falling for nice women. Nice women don't lie, cheat, steal, act violent or mean, destroy people or property, get you in trouble, or take you. Nice women are the kind you could take home and introduce to you family without giving your parents a heart attack.

2. Never fall in love quickly or blindly (and usually the two go together). When you go out with a woman, assume she's not perfect (like all of us). If she appears to be perfect, and if you intend to keep seeing her, start checking her out immediately. There's nothing worse than ugly surprises about your beloved after you're already in love.

3. Make sure the woman you're dating is honest. Find out if she lies to other people. If so, chances are she'll lie to you too. In order to have a good relationship, you have to be able to trust the person you love.

4. Always find out if a new woman is responsible and trustworthy. Never marry someone you wouldn't trust to feed your guppies and water your plants while you're away.

5. Meet her friends. Does she have any? Women without friends of both sexes are definitely suspect. Try

to talk to her friends in private. What do they say about her? Listen to them. Believe them.

6. Is she friends with her ex-boyfriends, ex-husbands, etc.? Or has she done something unforgivable? What?

7. Listen to her. Not only is this good for your relationship, but you could learn something very important. If she says, "I'm not good to fall in love with," then don't. Why would she lie to you?

8. Check her stability. Has she lived in the same place for any length of time? Does she pay her bills? Does she borrow money all the time? Does she drink, use drugs, spend money, or gamble uncontrollably?

9. Is she dangerous? Could she get you arrested, hurt, beat up, or killed?

10. Does she show up when she says she will or call if she's going to be late? Does she make plans ahead of time?

11. Can you count on her to be there if you need her? Or is she too busy needing you?

If you come up with the wrong answers to too many of the above questions, then dump her fast—even if you're so lonely you can't stand it and she's the only woman you know in the whole world. Do it right away before you really get hurt. If you find yourself needing the excitement that witches, bitches, and crazy ladies bring into your life, take up skydiving.

But what if you're not certain? What if you suspect she may be a bitch but you really can't tell for sure, and besides, she has lots of redeeming qualities? Then you need some survival strategies.

Bitch Survival Strategy

A woman's slight leaning toward bitchiness can be corrected, but only if you're very strong right from the beginning, and only if she's not a crazy lady.

Almost every woman has the ability to be a bitch. It's inside her, just beneath the surface, and shows its ugly head whenever you let it. If you never let it out, then it fades away. But just once let her get away with being a bitch to you and that's the way life is going to be with her.

A woman often decides how she's going to behave toward a man based on a "no guts" call. She's testing you from the beginning. You take her to a party and she flirts outrageously with someone else. You, being a perfect gentleman, never say a word. You don't call her aside and stand up for yourself by saying, "Hey, I brought you. You're my date. You wanna date him, make a date. But not on my time."

So she flirts some more and you still don't object, figuring you've got a chance to get laid tonight as long as you don't start a fight. Well, even if you do get a little, this is definitely a time when the fucking you'll be getting won't be worth the fucking you'll be getting.

A woman wants a man who is bold and ballsy enough to stand up for himself, to make sure he gets treated right, and to make sure she doesn't walk all over him. No woman wants a doormat. She wants a man who thinks enough of himself not to let her treat him badly.

A man at one of my seminars suddenly realized exactly when his perfect relationship went sour. "She said she'd come over and help me with my garage sale at eight in the morning and didn't show up until after noon. 'Oh, that's okay,' I said like a dummy. 'It's no problem.' From that moment on she walked all over me, and now I can see how it was my fault. I taught her that it was okay to treat me that way because I didn't say it wasn't."

Even if you don't care that she's late, or flirting, or putting you down, don't let her get away with it. By letting a basically nice woman get away with treating you badly, you can actually teach her to be a bitch. If the woman is already a bitch, let her get away with something once and she'll treat you like all the rest of the poor slobs in her life.

By calling her on the first indiscretion in a calm but firm manner, you'll feel better about yourself. And she'll feel better about you because she'll know you value yourself too much to be a doormat. If she's a borderline bitch or just trying bitchiness on for size, she'll be apologetic, and maybe even appreciative that you care enough to say something. She'll probably never try it again, although she may try something else and you'll have to call her on that too.

Loving a woman doesn't mean letting her treat you like dirt. This is truly a situation where you have to love yourself in order for her to love you.

Calling a woman on her bitchy behavior right away also saves you heartache later on. A man will often put up with bad behavior until it becomes unbearable, and then suffer through the pain of a breakup. So if you put your foot down immediately, the worst that can happen is that she'll be gone before you've fallen for her. There's even the possibility, if she's not a dyed-in-the-wool bitch, that she'll come back entranced by you, the one man she couldn't make jump through hoops.

If you've had a string of witches, bitches, and crazy ladies and you aren't sure what you want, the Man Power Method will help you find and keep the right kind of Ms. Right.

Crazy Love and the 12 Laws for Sane Love

Crazy love is when you do something crazy to make a woman fall for you. It usually doesn't work, because any sane woman thinks to herself, "Let me get this nut out of my life as quickly as possible." Or worse, she thinks, "He's crazy, and I certainly don't want to get too involved, but maybe he'll be useful."

Crazy love makes you wonder if she really loves you, and you do crazy things to make sure she does. You figure that if she isn't telling you to get lost, you have a chance. But she'll probably never be that blunt—because she either doesn't have the guts, doesn't care to make a scene, or likes the attention but has no intention of ever getting really close to you.

Instead, she tells you things like "I don't know what I want right now. I need time to think." Or, "I really (am fond of) (do care about) you." Or, "You're a (good friend) (nice person)."

She's late a lot or breaks dates often, and hardly ever has time to see you. When you *are* together, it's never long

19

enough and you never quite seem to have her full attention. She's indifferent, while you hang on her every word,
her every hello and good-bye, as if they were some indication that she's thinking about loving you or even beginning to.

You quash any thought that you may be wasting your
time by remembering some pittance of hope she's thrown
you. You fantasize about the perfect life the two of you
could have together. You write scripts in your mind of
what she says and what you say. Of course, when you get
together, she never says anything like your fantasy. That's
why you sometimes get more satisfaction from the relationship when you're apart than when you're together.

But do you really have a chance? Can you capture this
beautiful but elusive butterfly? Are you sure you want to?

Crazy love is always unbalanced. One of the people in
the relationship—you—is always willing and able to give
more love, while the other person may not even be worthy of the love you have to give.

The terrible part of crazy love is that the more you give
of yourself, the less she gives in return. When you respond
to her indifference with love, she learns how little she has
to do to get your love. Just to see if she can give even less,
she does. You become more desperate, and you respond
with more love, more gifts, more offers. So she gives back
even less and less. Like a business deal that goes sour, or
a losing ball game, this downward spiral is hard to stop
once it has started.

In case you're not sure where to draw the line between
being in love and being in crazy love, here are some
examples of what *not* to do. These are true stories of men
in love and of some of the unproductive schemes they
hatched, followed by the sane love laws they violated.

If you recognize yourself here, if you're caught in any
of the types of crazy love described below, or if your love
is just generally unrequited—stop. Don't rationalize that
your particular love problem doesn't exactly fit one of the

descriptions that follow. Just stop whatever you're doing.
Crazy love can make you come across as desperate,
needy, or downright nutty. That's no way to appeal to a
woman.

Crazy love inevitably makes you break one of the 12
important Sane Love Laws. Here are the 12 laws and the
stories of men who violated them.

Dual Decadence

"When I noticed how much she liked to drink, I figured
that was something we could really get into together. I
became her bartender, making her every fancy drink that
existed. I plied her with food and drink, and even drugs.
Our time together became an eating, drinking, drugging
orgy, followed by whatever sex act we could think of," a
wealthy bachelor, currently in a drug rehab program, told
me as he was trying to put his life back together.

"I was sure she would never find anyone like me who
would match her urge to indulge, urge for urge. You can't
imagine how shocked I was when she announced she was
going on the wagon and wouldn't be able to see me anymore because it was part of her therapy.

"I gave her love, sex, booze, and drugs—more drugs
than I could afford. And yet she left me. I heard she married someone who is a "born-again" and that they are
active in the church. How's a guy supposed to know what
a woman wants and what she doesn't want?"

Love Law #1:

**When two people form a relationship, each one
should improve his or her life. If life gets worse, or
you drag each other down, eventually one of you
wises up and splits.**

Financial Aid

"On the first date I showed up with my new car, a bouquet of flowers, and swept her off to the fanciest restaurant in town. On the second date I showed up with more flowers, candy, and a gold chain, just to show I cared. On the third date I took her shopping on Rodeo Drive for a new outfit. I taught her to appreciate the finer things in life," said a very lonely and frustrated stock analyst while relating how his attempts to buy love backfired.

"I paid her bills, lent her money, and took care of her, and so I figured she couldn't leave me unless she found someone richer who could take care of her better, which I didn't think would happen. I took her on fancy trips and doled out money whenever I got the chance. I knew there was no way she could afford to continue that lifestyle without me.

"But I began to see the transactional nature of the relationship, and I began to resent it. One day I show up without the flowers, presents, and big plans for the evening, just to see what would happen. She wonders what's wrong. Don't I love her anymore? *I* wonder what's wrong. How come women are always trying to take me?"

Love Law #2:

You can't buy love, and those who try never get their money's worth.

Jealousy

"I thought that if she was afraid she was going to lose me to another woman, that would make her rush into my arms," a Beverly Hills dentist confessed. "So I pretended to be having an affair with a very wealthy, very well-known woman in our town. I told my girlfriend that this woman called me all the time and kept propositioning me and proposing to me. I even bought myself gifts—shirts, golf clubs, seat covers for my car—and told my girlfriend that the other woman had bought them for me.

"At first, it worked. My girlfriend seemed really anxious to please, more than she ever had before. And she called me a lot. She even tried to compete in the gift-giving arena. And then, when my vacation came up, I told my girlfriend that this other woman was taking me to the Caribbean for a week. All of a sudden, she just told me that it was obvious the other woman made me much happier, so I should go with her. I was stunned, especially since the other woman didn't even know I was alive, but I couldn't back down and tell her the whole thing was a lie.

"Instead, I suggested that we should have an open relationship and both date other people. I said I wouldn't be jealous and that she could see whomever she liked and it was okay with me. Naturally, that didn't work either. She was hurt because I wasn't jealous, so she went out and found someone else who wanted an exclusive relationship."

Love Law #3:

Playing with jealousy is playing with fire. Somebody always gets burned. Women are jealous and insecure enough without you fanning the flames.

Me Tarzan

For more than one man I know, the feeling of falling in love is immediately followed by an uncontrollable urge to prove how macho he is. How lucky she is to have someone who is all man—part John Wayne, part Rambo, part Mario Andretti. One of my clients, a professional athlete, couldn't stop competing, even after the game was over.

"This guy in a bar was making a pass at her, you know, looking her up and down and making obscene little kissy noises at her. I wanted to show her that she'd never have to worry about guys like that again, so I slugged the guy. You'd think she would be appreciative, but she was all upset. Hey, I was brought up to protect the woman I love, I tell her, and what does she say? I'm a bully—and she hates the way I drive too!

"Now let me tell you, I once drove racecars. I always have a car under complete control, even when we're drifting through a high-speed curve. She's really safe with me, and does she appreciate it? No. Finally, she tells me she's not going to spend the rest of her life terrified, and leaves. And I was just trying to do the right thing."

Love Law #4:

Women like to imagine you would lay down your life for them, or race them to the hospital in an emergency. But only in their imagination. They don't really want the experience. A woman in love likes to feel that she has tamed the beast, not gotten stuck with one for life.

Becoming Indispensable

"I would do anything to show her how much I love her. I would kill to protect her. I would die for her, if she would only let me," a computer company executive said to me about a woman he had loved—sadly, in a platonic way—

for three years. He hoped to make her love him, but did exactly the wrong thing.

"I'm there whenever she needs me. If her checkbook doesn't balance, I'm her accountant. If her car doesn't work, I'm her mechanic. If her cat brings home a dead bird, I'm the dead-animal pickup. If her cleaning lady doesn't show, I'm the janitor.

"Whenever she needs advice about anything, she calls me. When she needs a last-minute escort, I'm always available. When other guys treat her badly, she can always cry on my shoulder. She depends on me. I know she needs me, but I don't know if she loves me."

Dependence can be love, of a sort, but it's not a healthy love. Sooner or later the dependent woman becomes angry at the man she depends on. He has taken away her ability to function in the world, and she will get even with him eventually. One way, of course, is by withholding what she knows he wants most—love and sex. If this sounds like something you'd like, if having a woman lean on you for everything appeals to you, adopt a pet and try to sublimate with other care-giving activities.

If you try to make a woman totally dependent in order to bind her to you, you will always lose, even if you succeed. Success simply means you'll get stuck with a woman who can never do anything for herself. Losing means she uses you for whatever you can do for her and falls in love with someone else, someone harder to get, more elusive, who appears to be more of a prize, and who is probably not nearly as nice as you.

Love Law #5:

In a healthy love relationship, you are equally dependent on each other.

Prove It

"If she really loves me, she would prove it by being the kind of woman I need," a client said to me about his new relationship. "She says if I loved her I wouldn't run around or fool around when I'm out of town on business. She wants to be married. I don't understand why we can't just live together as man and wife."

If you ask the woman you love to do something extraordinary to prove she loves you, she may leave. Not because she doesn't love you, but because she thinks you're crazy to ask such a thing.

Love Law #6:

Love doesn't demand proof from the beloved. It gives proof to the beloved.

Professor Higgins

"I'm a giver. I can't help myself," an account executive at a large PR firm told me. "I meet a woman and I feel sorry for her; I can see that there's really a very smart, very lovely person inside that I could bring out. So I change a basically nice, but not particularly debonair, woman into a sophisticated, well-dressed, educated, and traveled person, and then suddenly she doesn't need me anymore. It's as if she graduates. She takes her diploma and says good-bye, usually by running off with someone else." Actually, I've heard this same story over and over in different versions.

Who could ever forget Professor Higgins teaching Liza Doolittle to say "The rain in Spain" with a proper accent, dressing her, turning her from a street urchin into his fantasy English lady. Well, it's a good story, but it's a lot of work and rarely lasts.

Love Law #7:

When you change a woman into a different person, you have to take a chance that the new woman won't want you.

Suicide Threats

A commodities broker, already unhappy, came to me about his devastating love affair. "I always thought that being in love would make me happy, and it did for a while, but then I got depressed again. I worried all the time about whether we were okay, about whether or not she really loved me, about whether I could make enough money to keep her happy.

"I began driving her crazy, asking her over and over again if she loved me. I needed to hear her say the words over and over. We'd go along and everything would be all right, and then I'd sink into a terrible feeling of despair. She'd try to cheer me up and then give up. Finally, one day she said she thought I'd be happier with someone else.

"I was so depressed I told her I would kill myself if she didn't stay with me. She stayed for a while, but only long enough to see that I wasn't really going to kill myself, and then she moved out, leaving me with the name of her therapist 'in case of an emergency.' "

Love Law #8:

Depressed people are hard to love. Love should make you feel good, but having another person in your life

doesn't guarantee you'll be happy. Only you can make yourself happy, or sad.

Obsessive-Compulsive Love

"I've totally embarrassed myself by falling compulsively in love. I think about her day and night. If I turn on the radio in my car, all the songs are about her. If my phone rings, I pray that she's calling. She hardly knows I exist. I think I'm losing my mind," a schoolteacher said to me about the woman he loved.

"I know I'm acting weird but I can't stop. I see her everywhere. I chase strangers driving down the street or walking into an elevator. I spy on her and drive down her block a lot. I even call her on the phone and hang up just to hear her voice, or even her answering machine. I spend all my spare time trying to get close to her, questioning people who know her. I know she's getting annoyed instead of loving me back."

Obsessive-compulsive love is usually unrequited love: the loved one is afraid to love you back because then you'd really go crazy.

Love Law #9:

A woman wants to think she's loved by an elusive prince, not a desperate nut.

Instant Marriage

"It was love at first sight. I knew the minute I saw her that I would marry her. I asked her to marry me at the end of our first date. She said she'd think about it and I could tell she was impressed," a sales manager for an automobile parts company told me, explaining how he was trying to rush a woman he loved to the altar.

"I began to date her up so I'd be sure she wasn't seeing anyone else. We made plans for every holiday and vacation, going several years into the future. And she agreed. But then I began to get a sense that she wasn't as committed as I was. So I insisted we move in together and that we spend more time together. In three weeks we were formally engaged, but it was about then I could tell she was getting cold feet.

"She began working late, and making excuses for us not being together all the time, like she had to go shopping with her mother or she was having lunch with a girlfriend. Or she had a dentist appointment.

"So in order to bind her to me more, I went out and bought her a very expensive diamond engagement ring, thinking that would do the trick. She accepted the ring, but didn't spend more time with me. She seemed less committed than ever to our relationship.

"So, to help work things out, I took her to my therapist, and after two sessions of therapy, she gave me back my ring and told me I was smothering her."

Since relationships, like business deals, either get better or get worse, always start on a low romantic note. Then you have somewhere to go. Always start out just giving a little, then you have so much more to give later. Also, by starting slowly you have time to discover whether the woman you've found is worthy of the love you have to give.

Many men have a problem starting slowly. They tell me, "Listen, I know that's good advice for the average guy, but I've got a business I'm trying to build. I'm putting in eighty hours a week. I just don't have time for slow courtship." The answer here is the same as in business: you just have to find the time. We live in an age of instant gratification. You can get instant gourmet microwave dinners, but there's no such thing as instant love. If you think you've found it, it's usually instant lust, or runaway fantasizing. If you're serious about finding a life partner, you're going to have to invest some time. This book will help you make sure that that time is invested wisely and efficiently.

Love Law #10:

Rushing into love means rushing out of love even faster.

Suffering for Love

"It was so nice in the beginning, I didn't want to be the first to start an argument. So I never said anything when she did things that bothered me," a pre-med student said to me about the relationship he'd just ruined. "At first, it was little things. She'd break dates or come late. And I'd say, 'Oh, don't worry about it. No harm done. It's okay.' I thought she'd see how easygoing and flexible I could be.

"Then she started taking me more and more for granted. I took her to a party at the hospital where I worked, and she flirted with several of the men I work with. I tried to tell myself she was just outgoing, but inside it was eating me up. Then I heard she was dating someone I'm very good friends with. I was furious. When I told her, she said, 'Oh, I didn't think you'd care.'

"Three months later she was back, and I took her back. And now the whole thing is starting over again with the same problems."

Love Law 11:

Once a woman has learned that it's okay to treat you badly, it's hard to convince her otherwise

Doing Too Much

"I couldn't stop myself," Charles, a painting contractor, told me. "I was consumed with thinking of things to do to bind her to me. Because of her job, she was always traveling, but I wanted her to be thinking about me all the time, so I was always doing things for her, or devising some scheme to show her how much I loved her.

"First I started sending flowers to every place she was visiting, but she said that embarrassed her with her boss. So then I hired a whole Mariachi band to serenade her at her apartment one evening when she got home from a trip, but that got her in big trouble with the neighbors. She said the band stunk anyway. So I thought I'd better stay with what I know. In exchange for some housepainting, I got a friend with a body shop to paint her car as a surprise birthday present. He did a great job, but she didn't like it at all. Said it was the wrong color. While I was having it repainted, the rental car I got her broke down twice. So then I tried to make up for all my mistakes. I asked her mom what were her favorite colors, and on her next long trip, I had my best people repaint her whole apartment. Instead of being happy, she was furious. Said I invaded her privacy.

"She really told me off. Said it was weird for me to do all that stuff, and even if she loved me, which she didn't, she wouldn't stay with me because I'd never let her do anything for herself. Can you imagine that?"

Love Law # 12:

When in doubt over what action to take in a relationship, do nothing. Simply wait until the best course of
action comes to you. You can't blow it by doing nothing, especially if what you are going to do is a lot of
trouble and/or costs a lot of money and/or makes you
seem too eager.

CHAPTER THREE

Choosing the Woman Who's Right for You

The Man Power Method for finding and keeping the woman of your dreams is foolproof. Women around the world have used it to get the men of their dreams. Men have already begun to use it successfully.

By using the Man Power Method you will get the woman you want, but you must be careful whom you target with these techniques. You could wind up with the wrong woman too much in love with you. Your personal Woman Plan will help make sure you find the woman who's right for you.

Once you have mastered the techniques, they will work for you no matter what you look like or how bad your track record is, as long as you don't repeat the mistakes of the past with the same impossible woman. Forget everything else you have tried. You will be tempted to do the same things you did before—to make too many crazy phone calls, to blurt things out without thinking, to lay your heart on a platter for her to gobble up before you find out whether she deserves it or not, to fall for someone

33

you know is a classic witch, bitch, or crazy lady—hoping the Man Power Method will bail you out. Don't! Find the right woman this time.

Even if you think you know exactly the woman you want, take a few minutes to make out your personal Woman Plan, even if you just do it in your head. If you already have the right woman, you'll know immediately. If you don't, you may want to make some changes before you invest a lot of effort into making the wrong woman fall in love with you. Maybe you haven't met a woman who fits what you've been looking for because you don't know what you want or need.

You wouldn't go shopping for a new suit or a new pair of shoes or a new computer without knowing what you wanted. You'd know what color and style were appropriate for a suit, what weight material, and how much you wanted to spend. If you planned to buy shoes, you'd also know the style, color, and price, and what you'd wear them for. Before buying a computer, you'd probably do even more research, especially since it costs so much. You'd also know what you didn't want.

Why not do as much preparation and research about the next woman in your life? Don't just grab the next one you happen to meet. Be prepared, have a Woman Plan.

Women who filled out a Man Plan before they went looking for the right man have told me that they were able to find exactly the man they wanted and needed, even down to the fact that he was wearing a plaid shirt and khaki pants. Writing down exactly what you want in a woman will put you on the path to finding that woman.

In order to accomplish any goal in life, you have to know what the goal is; you have to have it pictured clearly in your mind. Consider your Woman Plan as relationship goal planning. Once you have a clear picture of the woman you need and want, the one who is best for you, you will be able to find her. When you have a Woman

Plan, you will never again have to wonder whether a woman is right for you. You'll know immediately.

Like many men, you might think you can choose from all the available women in the world. Unfortunately, there are probably things you don't like about at least 80 to 90 percent of the women you meet. So we're dealing only with the other 10 to 20 percent of available women who might meet your criteria.

A love plan will save you time. You won't have to sort through all the women in the world to find the 20 percent who might interest you. You can focus your efforts instead of chasing after hot numbers with short fuses.

Being Selective

My friend Margo said I should call this book *Smart Men, Foolish Penises.* In some cases, she's not far off. I've counseled many men who, in describing their chronic problems with women, use the identical expression, "just following my cock around."

When promiscuity wasn't as dangerous as it is today, sex often came first; and then either a relationship developed or it didn't. The "genitals first" approach to finding true love has never been very efficient, but for a while at least, it was fun and reasonably safe.

Times have changed, and probably you have too. Today there are powerful reasons to be selective. Chasing every tight skirt you see isn't just tacky. By scattering time, money, and energy in this way, you put yourself way behind the guys who are focused on getting ahead in today's competitive business environment.

If you're looking for a life partner, play it smart. The part of your anatomy to use first is your head. Use the Man Power Method and the "chemistry" will follow without fail.

Your Requirements

Right now, you may not know too much about your requirements. You may have thought, "I need a woman, any woman who's halfway good-looking, one who'll love me and who I'll love." It's not that simple. You'll soon realize how many requirements you really do have.

If you already have a woman you want to spend the rest of your life with, and you're absolutely sure she's the right one for you, skim this chapter and skip to chapter five, "Why Women Love." If you aren't absolutely certain you've already found the woman that's best for you, read on.

If you really want to be happy and in love with the right woman, a woman who will love you back, you have to know what's right for you in a woman. The Man Power Method will help you figure that out. The Man Power Method's first step is making a Woman Plan. This systematic approach to selectivity has worked for everyone who has used it. And it can work for you.

The process of making a Woman Plan is accomplished in three steps: first, you collect all your fantasies; second, you decide which of them you've got to have and which you can leave behind; and third, you test and refine the plan by doing some smart dating.

Visualizing Your Fantasy Woman

If you can visualize yourself doing something, the chances of your accomplishing that thing are greatly enhanced. In fact, recent discoveries in medical science point toward visualization as a way to improve our health and even cure disease.

Imagining the relationship you want is no different from imagining the career track you want to take or the tennis game you want to play or the golf swing you're trying to develop. Visualization is a powerful tool. Visualizing your ideal woman in writing will ultimately help you find her.

Buy a special notebook just for your Woman Plan. Writing it down not only helps the visualization process but also helps give reality to what is at present only imaginary. And the more specific you make your Woman Plan, the better.

You can either write spontaneously about the woman of your dreams or, if that seems difficult, simply fill in the spaces on the Woman Plan form starting on page 39.

Your Woman Plan starts out as a fantasy profile of the woman of your dreams. In the beginning, put down whatever comes into your mind first. Don't worry if it sounds outrageous or contradictory, silly or sexist. Just put it down. Nobody but you ever has to see what you've written. Don't worry about contradictions. Sure, you want an independent woman who sews, cooks, cleans, and wants lots of babies. We all want contradictory qualities. That's what makes finding a mate so difficult.

The important thing is to get all your "dream woman" fantasies on paper. You can refine your Woman Plan later.

In order to make your Woman Plan, you'll need some quiet time. Relax. Play your favorite music, turn on the answering machine, pour yourself a drink, and imagine you're about to plan for the biggest investment of your life—a woman you want to spend the rest of your life with.

Start with your first honest impulses. Here are some questions to get you started.

Does she look like Marilyn Monroe? Jacqueline Bisset? The girl next door?

If you're not getting a clear fantasy picture, think about the women in your past who really turned you on. (They reflect your real-life preferences rather than your fantasies, but that's okay too.) What were their common features? Did they tend to have blue eyes? Long hair or short hair? Were they all tall? Short? Slim or rounded? Natural types or carefully coiffed and made up? Casually dressed or elegantly outfitted? Did they wear jewelry? Glasses? Have you been attracted to "leggy blondes" or "petite brunettes"? Think about it. Almost every man has definite preferences. Indulge yourself in them right now. Write them down.

Just make sure your physical preferences don't make your search totally impossible. You may be one of the men who likes only really tall women, but if you're under five-seven, you have to realize that your insistence on tip-toppers is going to make finding love more difficult.

Does the woman of your dreams like to stay home or go out dancing? Does she like to go to new restaurants? To the theater or concerts? Does she like rock, classical, or country music? Does she watch television, play cards? Belong to civic or social groups? Does she drink? Smoke? Use drugs?

Is she a hot number? A happy homemaker? An executive, lawyer, doctor, or entrepreneur? What does she like to talk about? What are her hobbies? What does she like to do for fun?

What's most important to her? Her career? Her home? Her love life? In what order?

Is she involved in strictly women's interests—cooking, cleaning, taking care of children, clothes, etc.—or does she leave the house every day to work at a regular job? Does she work for herself or someone else? Does she travel in her job? How does she dress for work—in a business suit or more casually? Does she have a job that she does at home? Is she artsy? Creative?

Has she been married before? Does she have children? Does she want to have children with you? Does she like animals? Does she do all the housework, do you divide it, or do you have professional cleaning help?

How smart must she be? Does she have to be a college graduate, a high school graduate? Does she read a lot? What are her favorite books?

Is she religious? Does she belong to a particular church?

Is she spiritual? Does she believe in new-world philosophies or old-time religion? What are her political beliefs?

Imagine your life together. Where will you live? Your
place or hers, or a new place you choose together? Will
you have children?

Let your mind wander, and if you're not sure of the
answers to some of the questions, try various ones in your
imagination to see how they feel. Imagine yourself living
in the city and then in the country. Which makes you
more comfortable?

The idea is to get your thoughts on paper fast this first
time, using your first reactions and gut instincts. Use the
form on the following page or not, as you wish, but be sure
to put all your cherished fantasies into this first-draft
Woman Plan.

Personal Woman Plan Form

Looks, Finances, and Job

The woman of my dreams is _____ tall. She has
_____ eyes, _____ hair. She is _____ years old.
She has a _____ figure.

Her work is (very), (not very) important to her. She is
in the _____ business. She is (somewhat), (very), (not
very) creative. She feels (strongly), (not so strongly) about
her work. She makes _____ a year. She has a (conservative), (relaxed) approach to money matters. Her work
takes her out of town (often), (never), (sometimes).

Politics

She is a political (liberal), (conservative), just (left) or
(right) of center. She votes (sporadically), (religiously), for

(Republicans), (Democrats), (issues), (candidates). She is politically (active), (inactive).

Religion

She is a (practicing), (nonpracticing) _____. She goes to (church), (synagogue), (other). She goes to a religious service (sometimes), (regularly), (often).

Marital History

She (has), (has not) been married before. She has _____ ex-husbands and we (are), (are not) friends.

Children

She (has), (doesn't have) children from a previous marriage. They (do), (do not) live with her. She wants _____ children with me. She feels she (must have), (could live without) children.

Personal Habits

She wears (old sweats), (jeans), (pretty dresses) around the house. She is a very (sporty), (formal) dresser. She enjoys (staying home), (going dancing). She drinks (often), (once in a while) (hardly ever), (never). She (is), (isn't) a smoker. She (does), (doesn't) use recreational drugs. She spends (a lot), (hardly any) time alone. She has (lots), (a few) friends. She spends (a lot of), (very little) time with her female friends. She has (a few), (no) platonic male friendships.

Hobbies

She (is), (isn't) athletic and is (rarely), (often) involved in sports. Her favorite sport is _____. On a Sunday afternoon, she likes to (lay around and read), (go jogging), (work in the garden), (watch sports).

She (is), (isn't) the intellectual type and prefers (classical), (popular) music. She (does), (doesn't) like pets.

Personality Type

She is (sensitive and caring), (a rugged individualist), (a team player). She (does), (doesn't) put other people first. She (always), (almost always) puts me first.

Sample Woman Plan

What follows is a first-draft Woman Plan I borrowed from a man at one of my seminars, done without the help of the above form.

"My dream woman is very tall, six feet or more, with creamy white skin and long red hair. She is very slim, muscular, and athletic, and has a round tight ass and great breasts, small but erect. On a scale of one to ten, she is an eight or nine. She is very energetic and imaginative in bed, always willing to do whatever I want whenever I want, and almost insatiable, but she comes easily and often. She enjoys oral sex and is willing to try new positions and new ideas, but she is faithful and monogamous.

"She is my best friend, willing to listen and to encourage me when I feel down. She may have been married before but has no children from her previous marriage. She wants to have at least one child, maybe two, with me.

"She is a professional and has a good position with a corporation or large company. She goes to work every day and makes at least fifty thousand dollars a year. Our two salaries together allow us to have a very comfortable life-style—new cars, trips, club memberships, and a nice home.

"We attend church regularly and belong to the right groups. She takes pride in her appearance but isn't the type to spend every weekend in the beauty parlor or overindulge in makeup. She is a natural beauty and looking good comes easy for her. She has a great sense of humor and laughs easily. She doesn't take life too seriously, but she is sensitive, warm, and nurturing when necessary.

"We play tennis and golf and go to the beach in the summer. In winter we ski. She is outgoing and makes friends easily wherever we go. She drinks just a little. We enjoy singing together and playing backgammon and bridge. She's a good sailor and we belong to a yacht club.

"She's a good sport, very trustworthy, honest, never sulky and depressed. She's not interested in collecting expensive jewelry or spending time at the health spa.

"We mutually decide on investments and vacations, but she is generally in charge of household things and I take care of our mechanical things like the cars.

"When we first meet, I can tell she's interested in me, but she plays it cool. We date several times before we go to bed, but then it's wonderful and we're together from then on. She thinks I'm very handsome and can't keep her hands off me. We have a big wedding, and honeymoon in the Virgin Islands."

How's that for a demanding Woman Plan? Inconsistent? Definitely not what you'd want? Obviously. Each Woman Plan is individual, intentionally selfish, and private.

Like every first attempt at a Woman Plan, this man's plan changed as he began to date. He decided certain traits were too difficult to find and not so important as he had originally thought. He realized he could like a woman who was less than six feet tall, so he was able to to revise his Woman Plan and open up his horizons. As he used his plan, it became more flexible, more realistic, and open to many more women.

"For the first time in my life," he told me, "I wasn't just groping aimlessly, not knowing what I was looking for. My dating became more goal-oriented. I knew what I was looking for in a woman, and it was definitely more than the good time I used to settle for."

His Woman Plan worked, and the woman he married is almost exactly like the one described in his original plan, except that she's five-six and has long brown hair instead of long red hair. You'll be surprised how close to your dreams you can come.

Before You Get Serious

There are some important questions you should answer about any woman you're thinking of getting involved with. You may want to use these questions to refine your first-draft Woman Plan, before you start to use it.

IS SHE REALLY READY TO COMMIT, OR AM I WASTING MY TIME?

If you find Ms. Perfect and fall madly in love, only to find out that a committed relationship has no place in her life for the next ten years, you're going to be very unhappy. Before you fall for her, there are ways to tell whether she's ready to settle down.

First, find out if she is *capable* of maintaining long-term relationships or attachments. Has she made and kept commitments in the past? Has she been married before, gone steady, lived with a man, or been engaged? For how long? Does she have roots? A home? A long-term lease? Pets? Plants? Old friends? A lifetime gym membership?

Women with no roots are generally a bad bet for a serious relationship. Some are really neurotic, some are just flaky, and some are simply young, wild, and crazy. A few are simply waiting to buy furniture when they find the right man. Often they are career women, and though stable, mature, and capable of maintaining a committed relationship, they have promised themselves to put their careers first, at least for a while.

So how do you know if a woman who is *capable* of making a commitment is *ready* to do so? Women who want to be married talk about weddings, they invite you to friends' weddings, they throw showers, they are brides-maids, and they gurgle at every baby they pass. Age has a definite influence on whether a woman is ready for marriage and commitment. A woman of thirty or thirty-five is much more likely to be ready than one of twenty or twenty-five.

WHY BUY THE COW WHEN MILK IS SO CHEAP?

It's been a confusing thirty years. In the 1950s, a guy could assume that what a woman wanted was marriage, home, and kids. Then came free love, then feminism, and now your boss at the office is a woman. What the hell do women really want?

Don't listen to what anybody says, least of all the women you go out with. When a woman is ready, willing, and able to commit to a man, she wants to get married. Busy, independent lady executives eventually find time to fit a husband into their lives. Even woman rock stars finally get married.

So if your Woman Plan calls for a modern, hip woman who is mad about you and happy to live with you, but doesn't care about getting married, someone's got to tell you: You've got a fair chance of making the deal, but about nil chance of having it hold.

Eventually, couples who live together without getting married either capitulate and go to the altar or they break up. The reasons are various. In a family emergency, is a "live-in" part of the family council or is she just a girlfriend? If you are in an accident, she has no legal right to speak for you and may not even be allowed to visit you in the hospital. Deep down, no matter what she tells you, she yearns for the "till death us do part" commitment from you, particularly if she wants babies.

Meanwhile, you're spending a certain amount of energy fighting all society and worrying about your relationship. Why? Usually, all the stated reasons for flouting conventional marriage boil down to one thing: You want to keep your options open. You're not really ready to commit. Just remember: Eventually you'll have to marry or break up and start over with someone else whom you'll either have to marry or lose.

WHAT IF ONE OF US DOESN'T WANT CHILDREN?

Many women tell me, "Oh, I'm not going to have kids. I couldn't give them the attention they need and still pursue my career." At the time they're saying this, they really believe it. Then, five or ten years later, they are frantically buying pregnancy-test kits, taking their temperatures every morning, and trying desperately to get pregnant.

Every woman has a biological clock ticking away inside her. It has nothing to do with her plans or her lifestyle preferences. It's genetic. Imperceptible in her twenties, it starts ticking louder and louder in her thirties. Either she has a child or the clock pounds away, reminding her that she's approaching menopause without having reproduced.

If your Woman Plan calls for a woman who doesn't want

kids, you'd better be looking for a woman in her fifties or older.

COULD I CHANGE HER?

Leopards don't change their spots, and a woman is not likely to change herself dramatically just because you come into her life. That's one important reason why you are making a Woman Plan. It's worth taking the time to figure out what's important to you, because you're not going to find some attractive woman and then simply mold her to suit all your other requirements. Women come complete with beliefs, preferences, and habit patterns, just as you do.

When you meet a new woman, consider yourself an investigative reporter who needs to find out everything about her, your subject. Knowing a woman's past is the key to her future. People rarely make huge changes without years of therapy, so you can pretty much tell how a woman will behave in the future by knowing her past.

For example, to find out how a woman feels about making a commitment, ask her. "Have you ever been in love? Have you ever lived with anyone? How long were you together? Do you still see each other?"

If a woman is still friends with an ex, don't be dismayed. Actually, it's a good sign. At least you know she didn't do something so bad to him that he never wants to see her or hear from her again. A woman who has treated other men badly is bound to treat you badly.

Whenever possible, meet and talk to other men who've dated the woman you're interested in. Buddy to buddy, pal to pal, try to get them to level with you. The best recommendations are from ex-husbands or ex-boyfriends. Next come grown children, or even little ones. They know how Mom treats men and are often indiscreet enough to tell.

Find out about her parents. Does she love them both? And most important, how does her mother treat her father? Little girls first learn how to treat men from watching how their mommies treat their daddies.

WHAT IF I'M TURNED ON ONLY BY BEAUTY QUEENS?

When I help men make up a Woman Plan, I notice that the biggest, most consistent mistake they make is to focus exclusively on physical attributes. "I visualize a Marilyn Monroe type with long blond hair, big tits, cute little baby-doll rear, long tan legs, a suntan, big blue eyes, and pouty lips—and madly hot for me." Nothing else. A woman could be a convicted felon with an IQ of 67, but if she looks like Marilyn Monroe, she meets 100 percent of this man's Woman Plan.

Everyone, of course, is entitled to physical preferences. You may be one of the men who likes only very short women or athletic women or very glamorous types. If that's really important, then keep it in your Woman Plan. However, if your physical preferences have to do with blond hair, or even big breasts, remember that with modern science anyone can be blond or big-busted or blue-eyed.

By the way, beautiful women are very sensitive about being judged on their looks alone. A beautiful woman knows when a man is attracted only to her face or her figure and doesn't care at all about what's inside her brain or her soul.

"It makes me really angry," one very beautiful actress told me. "I'll be having a serious conversation with a man about an issue that's really important to me, and he'll be staring at my breasts in a way that I know he hasn't heard a word I've said. It's more than a little insulting."

Other, not quite as attractive women also resent being judged on their looks. "I notice how men sometimes look right through me, as though I don't even exist," an average-looking woman told me.

Another not unattractive woman told me, "I resent the attitude that you're nothing unless you're beautiful. If you're a woman and you don't look like Cher in a Holiday Spa commercial, the implication is that you're not valuable. And I'm fed up with guys who judge another man's success by how beautiful his wife is. I know some really beautiful women who sleep all day and use men for whatever they can get from them."

When you describe your dream woman, remember that no matter how good-looking she is when you marry her, eventually she'll get old. Her looks will begin to fade, and her personal qualities will be more important than ever.

How, you might wonder, does any red-blooded guy stay in love with a woman when she gets old and wrinkled and doesn't look anything like the beautiful girl he married? The answer is that when you are truly in love with a woman, and she loves you, you will always be able to look at her and see the beautiful girl you married, and she'll always be able to look at you and see the handsome young man she married. You'll always see yourself reflected in her eyes as a cute-assed young stud, no matter how old, gray, crotchety, and decrepit you've become—that's one of the real secrets of enduring love.

So get your physical preferences down, and then do some deep thinking about what else in your ideal woman will ensure real compatibility. It's entirely individual, but studies have given us one clue: Most people are most comfortable with their sociological equal and psychological opposite. In other words, someone with the same educational and social background. Not necessarily the same religious beliefs, but equal life values and standards. That means if you're college-educated, you should look for a mate with a college education. Your psychological oppo-

site means a woman who balances you out—an introvert
if you're an extrovert, an optimist if you're a pessimist.

WHY DO I FIND IT EASY TO LOVE A WOMAN BUT HARD TO LIVE WITH ONE?

The longer you've been single, the longer you've lived
alone, the longer you've had everything exactly your way
all the time, the harder it will be for you to find the
woman of your dreams. That's because you're more set in
your ways, and choosier. You have a more definite idea of
exactly what you do want and what you don't. You may
even find it easier to list the qualities you don't want in a
future mate than to list those you do.

Part of your plan, in fact, should include a short list of
characteristics—your personal reject list—that totally rule
out any hope of compatibility. Here's one man's sample
list. "No drug users, no cigarette smokers, no women with
kids, no feminists, no Republicans." A reject list will save
you a lot of time and trouble. When you meet women who
are initially attractive but fit one of your reject-list qualities, you'll be forewarned.

If one of these women is constantly in close proximity
because she's a coworker or neighbor, keeping hands off
is a little trickier, especially if she's sexy and attracted to
you. You can be friendly with her—but absolutely no flirting, nothing even resembling a date, and, of course, no
screwing around. Just remember, you could miss meeting
the love of your life because you're busy having a fling
with someone you now know is hopelessly wrong for you.

Test and refine your Woman Plan by comparing it to
the women you date. The search strategy in the next
chapter will help you find and meet a lot of women so that
you can choose the one who's right for you.

Your Search Plan

"My mother always told me God would send me the right woman," a forty-six-year-old bachelor said at a recent workshop. "She said that one day, when I was least expecting it, the girl of my dreams would appear and everything would work out perfectly. Well, I've been waiting, and so far she hasn't appeared. What do you think I'm doing wrong?"

After explaining to him that God helps those who help themselves, I helped him make a search plan so that he could find a quantity of eligible women from which to choose. First, he had to leave the fairy tales and old wives' tales behind.

There are almost as many men waiting for Cinderella's glass slipper to fall in front of them as there are princesses waiting for Sir Galahad. Rapunzel probably won't lower her hair to you from the nearest corporate tower. If you want a princess, you'll have to be a prince to start with.

Even if you you are a prince, your modern-day princess probably won't leave a glass slipper for you to find. She's more likely to be on the tennis court wearing hard-to-lose Reeboks, or shopping at Neiman-Marcus in fancy Italian pumps.

In order to make your search plan effective, make a real commitment to the search. Be willing to spend time, money, and energy and be willing to meet a volume of women. There are good women out there, but like good jobs, the good women will go to the men who really try.

The Commitment to Search Seriously

Looking for a woman to spend the rest of your life with should be a conscious, organized, high-priority activity. You can trade in your computer or your car every few years, but not your mate. We're talking about a lifetime partner. This is not a casual undertaking. Next to taking care of yourself and your work, your search should be the most important thing in your life.

If you find that your tennis game or softball game or poker game is more important than searching for the right woman, perhaps you aren't really ready to make a lifetime commitment. If you are ready, push your search to the top of your priority list.

If you are seriously ready to settle down, make an agreement with yourself that you will stop chasing every strange woman who looks good, that this is the year you are going to get married to a wonderful person. Tell yourself that you know she's out there, just waiting for you to find her, and that you are going to search for her as if she were a prize worth a million dollars, because a good life partner is worth far more.

By devoting as much time to your search as you would to any other really serious activity, you will succeed. Without a real commitment, you will be lulled into hopeful passivity, fantasizing about the princess who providentially winds up on your doorstep or the dream girl you spot across a golden field (after which you run into each other's arms à la a Hallmark commercial). It's not just the handsome or rich men who succeed in finding the women they want, it's the dedicated men, the ones who really put themselves out and search in an organized, regular manner.

The seriousness and purposefulness with which you approach your task will also be noticed by the women you meet. They will be assessing how serious you are, how real you are, or whether you just want to fool around. A woman who is ready to settle down will naturally lean toward a man who is committed to finding a mate. It's a part of the natural propagation of the species.

Don't try to be cool by being indifferent to commitment. You'll only wind up with women who want to fool around, and while you're busy fooling around, the girl of your dreams may pass you by. Anyone can find a woman to fall in love with for a weekend, but we're talking about forever.

Erasing Mental Blocks That Keep You From Finding Love

I often start my seminars for men and women with an exercise in which I ask them to close their eyes and follow along with a fantasy even if it makes them uncomfortable. Then, as a goal-setting visualization, I have them imagine they are at their own wedding. To make it as real as possible, I ask them to picture where the wedding is taking place, what family members are present, who is in the wedding party, what they are wearing. I ask them to imagine they are hearing the wedding march. The men then visualize their bride coming down the aisle on the arm of her father. As they put the ring on her finger, they hear themselves pledge to love, honor, and cherish forever.

There are always at least three people in each group who are so uncomfortable they open their eyes immediately, unable even to begin. Then there are a few others who either burst out in uncontrollable laughter or shriek in horror at what they are visualizing—marriage and lifetime commitment.

If a past bad experience has sensitized you to marriage, if you fear failure, or if for any reason you can't imagine going through with marriage, you're no different from lots of men and women I meet. Affirmations are the cure.

Whatever reasons your subconscious has had for avoiding love or commitment, repeating positive love affirmations on a daily basis will help erase the old programming that may be keeping you from finding love. Here is an example of a general-purpose love affirmation:

I, (your name) _____, am loving and lovable.

I, (your name) _____, deserve a wonderful woman.

I, (your name) _____, am ready for a lasting, committed relationship.

I, (your name) _____, am ready to be happy in love.

Affirmations should be simple, easy to say and remember. They should be in the present tense and involve your name, or the pronoun *I*, or both.

It is best if you repeat your affirmation aloud, but saying it to yourself works too. The most important thing is consistency and repetition. At some time every day, perhaps while you're jogging or working out, or walking from the subway to your office, repeat your affirmation rhythmically, over and over, like a chant, until it becomes part of your subconscious.

With your Woman Plan in hand and your attitude positive, you are ready to find the girl of your dreams.

A Volume of Women

Your Woman Plan gives you a clear picture of your Ms. Right, but that doesn't mean she's going to be the first woman you meet.

In the beginning, test your Women Plan against all those women who appear to meet at least some of your Woman Plan requirements. Don't take them all out on fancy or expensive dinner/movie/dancing dates. It's a bad idea to spend too much money on the first date. You'll only be giving a woman the wrong idea and setting up unrealistic expectations on her part; spending a lot may also make it hard for a woman to reciprocate. A modest first date is a good way to find out if a woman likes you or merely where you can take her and what you can buy her. At first, try to get to know each new woman well enough to decide whether or not she matches some of your important Woman Plan requirements. If she does, take her out on a date, at least once.

By dating several women, you will develop self-confidence. You will also be able to refine your Woman Plan. By comparing different women, you will become more discerning in what you want and need in a relationship.

By practicing the Man Power techniques in this book, you will be successful with several women. Then you'll be in the position of selecting the woman you want, rather than taking whichever one says yes.

By having more than one woman, at least in the preliminary dating stages, you will appear more desirable to all women. Nobody wants to eat in a restaurant with no cars parked out front, and no woman wants a man nobody else wants.

Finding the Woman You Want

"So how do I get all these women?" you ask. By forgetting the old limits that have held you back. Let go of the pride that says, "I wouldn't let somebody fix me up." Or, "I'd never join a dating service." Or, "I'd never go out with someone I met at work."

If you wanted a new job, you wouldn't say, "I'm not going to use an employment agency." Or, "I don't want to let my friends know I'm looking." Or, "I'm not going to chase after newspaper ads." Knowing that a job's not going to appear by magic, you'd use all the means at your disposal to generate as many prospects as you could.

Finding the woman you want involves three categories of searching:

1. Open searching, which includes getting some help from your friends, as well as being open to chance encounters.
2. Volume searching, a professional approach for finding a lot of women.
3. Primary search activity, which automatically puts you in touch with the kind of women you want to meet.

By combining these search categories, you will have a proven strategy for obtaining a steady supply of new and interesting women. The idea is not to be dependent on any one category, or even two. It's up to you to pick at least one specific way to meet women in each of these categories. To help you decide, here are many frequently used methods, grouped by search category.

Open Searching

Open searching means more than just being passively open to chance encounters. To take advantage of opportunities to meet women, you must be prepared, and you must take the initiative.

Here are some specific ways of open searching. Try to use as many as you can.

THE "CUTE MEET"

In the movies, the "cute meet" happens when she backs her Jeep into his Porsche. Or they get stuck together on a ski lift. Or their shopping carts tangle at the supermarket.

Actually, you can meet women anywhere. You don't even have to get your Porsche dented. Bookstores are great places to meet and strike up a conversation. Department stores are loaded with women. There's nothing wrong with your local supermarket, even when the carts don't tangle. All single people go grocery shopping. Ms. Right could be the lady next to you at a red light, or standing in front of you waiting to get into a crowded lunch spot. Whatever the situation, always be friendly and open to encounters. Your own version of Hollywood's "cute meet" is open searching at its most open and unpredictable. Never quit trying, but don't count on the results.

AT WORK

If you happen to be in a position of power or influence, single women in the office will naturally be attracted to you. The impact of your Italian leather briefcase and Gucci shoes, your BMW and condo address, is definitely not lost on a woman who works at the law firm where you're a partner. On the other hand, you wouldn't want her to pick you just because you're rich and influential.

There's nothing wrong with being open to true love at the office, but be aware of the dangers. An office environment is rife with politics and hidden agendas. You may be sure that the new sales rep is crazy for you, only to be hit with a charge of sexual harassment. Or a hot romance could suddenly blow up in an emotional scene in the lobby, and you could lose your job as well as the girl.

A safer way to tap into the female population at a large company is to join a company-affiliated activity, such as a ski club. You'll meet women who are not your employees and are not even in your department, which is important. Romance is tolerated more easily by the company if it stems from one of these quasi-"outside" activities.

A word to the wise: Never expect to keep a romance secret. If you do start seeing someone from the company, preempt the rumor mill by letting your boss know that your intentions are "honorable."

SINGLES' BARS AND HANGOUTS

Sure, there are a lot of single women on a Friday night, but most of them are just out to have fun. A woman doesn't hang out at a bar to meet the man of her dreams. She goes to a bar to flirt, to see whom she can attract, maybe even to take someone home to fill a lonely evening but not to keep.

Casual sex is what singles' bars are all about. That's why they used to be fun, and that's why they're not now. Don't waste your time at one unless none of the other approaches listed here are available to you.

COED GYMS

Most women aren't looking for an Arnold Schwarzenegger, but almost all women appreciate a man who keeps himself trim. Besides, working out is good for you.

These days all kinds of women can be found in sweaty tights. You'll find some of the same on-the-make types who once prowled the singles' bars, but you may also find that special classy lady outlined in your Woman Plan. Be open to a chance encounter at a Nautilus machine. Most health clubs have a juice bar, giving you an opportunity for a minidate, which is usually the best first step with any woman.

CHURCHES

Many churches have organizations for singles. If you're already attending a church, check into it. If not, it's probably a mistake to act religious just to meet a woman.

There are few secrets in church, and everybody knows everything about everyone else. So if you do see someone in church you'd like to meet, it's easy to introduce yourself or arrange an introduction. If you like each other, you'll have a built-in support group for your relationship.

THE FIX-UP

This is probably the very best way to meet a compatible woman. You already know many of the same people and probably have similar values.

The problem with the fix-up is that it relies on friends who are busy and not even aware that you are searching. Take the initiative.

There's no reason to be embarrassed by asking your

friends to fix you up. Go through your address book and call all the people you know, men and women. Let them know at the very beginning of the conversation that you are ready to make changes in your life, that you are sincerely interested in settling down with the right woman. Tell them you're tired of fooling around. If you must, give the impression that you've done it all. That way, you won't feel as if you're admitting you can't get a date.

People who know you well will be best able to recommend someone to you. Try to be open to meeting almost anyone. Be flexible, not fussy and particular; don't say, "I only date *Playboy* centerfolds." Or, "My last girlfriend was a Phi Beta Kappa prom queen, gourmet cook, top-seated tennis player who was studying law at night." When your friends ask what you're looking for, tell them, "Just someone you think I'd like."

Volume Searching

You probably aren't interested in hanging out in a singles' bar waiting for Ms. Wonderful to come in, and you can't count on chance encounters. Referrals from friends may yield some high-quality dates, but not in the volume you need. In order to ensure that volume, use classified ads and dating services.

Almost every large city has dating services. They are often the best way for busy people to meet. If you have an impression that they are just a different kind of meat market, you'll be surprised at how sophisticated some have become, and you'll be pleasantly surprised at the quality of the people you meet. You can actually have women delivered to your door either on paper or on videotape, without anyone ever knowing what you're doing. Remember, you can't choose without knowing what's out there.

If you are in the highly desirable age range (there were hardly any men born in the U.S. from 1941 to 1945, the war years, so men born then are at a premium), by all means try the classifieds and the dating services. You'll be swamped. If you're in the surplus-male age range of under thirty, you may need a dating service just to find enough women to choose from.

Regardless of your preconceptions about the following ways of meeting women, be sure to include one in your overall search-plan strategy. Try it, you might like it.

CLASSIFIED ADS

Classifieds are a chance to show off your best attributes on paper and hide the rest. And that's just what your ad should do. After all, you wouldn't tell a prospective employee about the long hours when placing a help-wanted ad. Why write about your bad points?

Always advertise in the kind of publication the woman you want to meet would read. And the longer you make your ad, the more open you are about your requirements, and the more you tell about what you have to offer a woman, the more responses you will receive. I know one man who advertised that he was a gray-haired fox who liked to be romantic, always bought flowers, and opened doors for ladies. He was swamped with replies.

Be prepared to follow up right away if you get a letter you like. Send a picture and make contact. If she wrote to you, she may have answered other ads as well.

The problem with ads is that you never really know what the other person is like. People lie and send old photographs. The first meeting can be a shock, so make it a casual, brief date.

DATING CLUBS

Almost every major city has dating clubs. Some of them
have parties and simply let you mingle with other mar-
riage-minded singles. Others promise to send you information on a specified number of computer-selected
matches each month until you find the woman of your
dreams.

If you join a dating club, join the most expensive one
you can afford. That way, at least you know the women
you meet were serious enough to have shelled out all that
money. They will also value you more if they meet you at
an expensive place. On the other hand, you will be automatically limiting yourself to only those women who can
afford to join the club.

Just joining the club isn't enough. You have to work at
it, reading through member profiles sent to you, not getting too blasé because there are so many women available, keeping interested when you've met three women
you hate all in a row.

VIDEO DATING

If you have no time to waste, try one of the more sophisticated, high-tech video dating clubs. Some of them will
send you videotapes of new women each month—without
your ever having to be videotaped yourself. Other clubs
will allow you to join only if you agree to be videotaped.
Almost all will allow you to join without revealing your
identity to the other members.

The advantage here is that you never have to be rejected in person. So she didn't like your videotape, so
what? At least you didn't have to look at her while she said
no.

Primary Search Activity

Since this is where you will be spending most of your planned searching time, your primary search activity should be something that is educational and/or fun for you. In addition to dating randomly, make a commitment to participate in an ongoing enjoyable activity that involves the kind of women you want to meet.

Review your Woman Plan and think about what organizations and activities your ideal woman would be involved in. A few of these should interest you too, and these will be your first candidates for a primary search activity.

You will be committing a lot of your spare time to this activity, so be sure it's something that you have a real interest in and that you'll enjoy. For example, you're sure to meet interesting women in the Sierra Club, but if you're "pro-use" or if you just don't like the outdoors, find another organization to join.

Be sure you do something that a lot of women are doing too. And I don't mean the "cheerleaders" who hang around the local softball league. Find an activity you can enjoy that attracts more women than men—the kind of women who are in your Woman Plan.

BUSINESS-ORIENTED ORGANIZATIONS

Most fields have a female-oriented organization that doesn't exclude men, for example, Women in Business or Women in Cable Television. You'll find many attractive, interesting women members. Offer to get involved and contribute your time.

CLASSES

Most universities have evening programs; skim through their catalogs and see what interests you. If you have a special field of experience or expertise, consider teaching at an extension or alternative-education school. You'll meet a constant flow of new women, and all eyes will be riveted on you for perfect "podium effect" (see page xx).

CLUBS, SOCIETIES, AND MUSEUMS

You'll find lots of women in political campaigns and civic organizations. If you have kids, check out your local Parents Without Partners organization. Call a nearby museum to find out what societies are affiliated with it. If you've always wanted to improve your public speaking, visit some local Toastmasters clubs. Other activities with a good female-to-male ratio include cruise ship vacations, gourmet cooking classes, seminars for self-growth, and beginning sports classes.

What Do You Say? The Approach

Do you go through agonies when approaching a strange woman for the first time? Most men do. The key to self-confidence in meeting a woman is to understand that she feels awkward too, even if she looks and acts very sure of herself.

How you approach a woman depends a lot on the non-verbal signals exchanged. The best first reaction when you see a woman who interests you is a friendly smile. A come-on from most women will be nothing more than a brief smile. Sometimes a longer-than-necessary glance is your only indication that there's some interest on her part. It's up to you to pick up on it.

Regardless of who initiates the eye contact and the smiling, it's important that you respond right away in a chance-encounter situation or the opportunity may be lost forever. Even if you're in a group that will be together for several hours, it's best to respond immediately. Most women won't continue to flirt or keep smiling, because of fear of rejection. If you do respond right away, you'll seem spontaneous (even if you're not). If you don't, she's liable to write you off as uninterested and/or a wimp.

To be able to respond immediately, it helps to be prepared. If you're like most of us, you can't count on being cute on the spur of the moment. But you don't want to just stand there, frozen, trying to figure out what to do, or mumble something lame, such as "Uh, do you have the time?" Have a stock question or line figured out for whatever setting you're in—something other than "Do I know you?" Figure it out *before* you spot the lady. Have it on tap. Here are some examples.

If you're shopping for groceries and you see a woman who attracts you, smile at her. If she returns your smile, ask her a grocery-related question, such as "Can you help me—is it basil or tarragon that goes on artichokes before steaming?" Think it through beyond the first question. You don't want her to just say "Basil" and then walk away, right? Have some follow-up lines on tap as well, such as "Actually, I don't even know how long to steam the damn things. What do you think?" If she has the answers, you might say, "I'd sure like another gourmet cooking lesson. My name is Sam Green, and I live in the neighborhood. Can we get together for coffee sometime?" If she doesn't have the answers, use a different follow-up line.

If you're driving and an attractive woman returns your smile, roll down your window at a red light and talk to her. Don't waste precious seconds thinking of something car-

or traffic-related for an opening gambit. Just use a stock line, such as "Hey, I'd like to stop and talk, but I'm late for a meeting. Can I call you for coffee?" (Grab something to write on *before* you get to the light.)

If you're at a party and you see someone you'd like to meet, see if you can catch her eye. If you can lock glances with her, smile a bit flirtatiously. If she smiles back, you don't need a cute line. Just walk up and introduce yourself: "Hi, I'm Tom Miller. Are you with anyone?"

If, on the other hand, a woman at the party has been giving you intense, flirtatious looks, the situation is different. She obviously wants to meet you, so you can get personal much faster. "How come you're such an outrageous flirt?" is a fun line that gets you into a bantering mode right away.

Big-city women and big-city situations are tough. If you're suddenly smitten by a woman bustling along Fifth Avenue in New York City, I know of no graceful way of approaching without her thinking she's in for an upscale mugging. You have a shot at it, though, if the setting is a department store. Be sure she returns your smile (and be prepared to buy something nice—for a sister, a niece, or a daughter), then simply ask, "Excuse me, I'm trying to find a [sweater, bag, whatever] for my niece, and I'm over my head. What would a twelve-year-old girl like? I'm afraid that clerk will sell me just anything."

If your big-city woman is waiting for a cab, offer to share a cab. If she's waiting for a table, offer to share a table (even if she's with a girlfriend). If she declines the table offer but gives you a big smile, seize the moment. "I work in the next building. My name is Bill Blank. [Stick out your hand.] What's yours?" Don't leer. Look straight into her eyes, and don't stare at her chest. A straightforward introduction coupled with a nice smile can disarm the most sophisticated lady.

In general, if you can't catch her eye, or she glares at

you, forget it. Who needs certain rejection? But if you connect with a look and a smile, go for it. Approach her. The worst that can happen is nothing—the same outcome as if you hadn't tried at all, except that now you've had some practice.

In a chance-encounter situation, suggest getting together for coffee, not drinks. It's not as overtly seductive and will sound safer to the woman. Don't make a definite date right then and there; if you do, you'll have no reason to need her number, right? I wish I had a nickel for every man who's been stood up sitting in a coffee shop at the appointed hour waiting for a woman who has only a face and a first name. Remember, women often chicken out on these things—even if they'd really like to see you again. So strike while the iron is hot; get her full name and phone number. "Let's have coffee—let me call you."

If you run out of conversational ideas after the first few exchanges, try a little self-disclosure combined with flattery. "You know, I just have a terrible time meeting people for the first time—and you're so attractive—it must be easy for you. . . ."

That's all you need to do—make contact. The Man Power Method will make the rest easy.

CHAPTER FIVE

Why Women Love

I 'll admit it, women love men for the craziest reasons. Men have always been mystified by why a particular woman chooses a particular man.

Why Women Love Jerks

Many women will throw themselves at a rich man, even if he's a jerk, and not just for the money. Power is the rich man's aphrodisiac. Women are drawn to all kinds of powerful men (rich men, politicians, even gangsters) because of genetic programming that' goes back to when a woman's survival and the survival of her children depended on having a powerful mate. If a woman is insecure or has no identity of her own, she's tempted to become Mrs. Senator, Mrs. Doctor, or simply Mrs. Rich Bitch, for security, if not for love.

There are lots of reasons why women love jerks. Sometimes women are attracted to weirdos or gangster types because their lives are dull and they need excitement, or because they feel more accepted by someone who's obviously lower down on the social or intellectual scale. At other times, a woman will stay with an out-and-out bastard because she feels that any man is better than no man, or because the bastard is sexy—the same reasons why men stay with witches, bitches, and crazy ladies.

Fortunately, most women are also susceptible to nice guys, especially those that have an intuitive sense of what makes a woman fall in love.

Why Women Love Nice Guys

Have you ever noticed how some men always seem to have a woman in love with them? Not a witch, bitch, or crazy lady, but a nice woman, one most men would do anything to have. And what's so great about this guy? Nothing. He's not particularly handsome, tall, rich, or powerful, and he doesn't always treat her as well as you would, yet she adores him.

The men I've known who were best at wrapping women around their little finger were neither rich nor powerful, neither outlaws nor bastards. What they did brilliantly and intuitively was to get on a woman's wavelength, communicate with her in a way that touched her soul, and give her the special attention that made her feel more understood and special than she had ever felt before. What these few lucky men did intuitively, you can learn to do easily and naturally.

I've watched in amazement as my friend Eric, a man who is attractive but not fantastic-looking, practically penniless, with a power quotient of almost zero, scores over and over again with the most sophisticated and desir-

able women. He's not the life of the party, not full of jokes
and clever repartee. He doesn't have muscles or a fancy
car and he's just okay in bed, yet time after time he gets
the girl.

He doesn't just get women, he possesses them. Women
call him and cook for him and shower him with gifts and
invitations. It's obvious he can have any woman he
chooses whenever he wants. Women yearn for him when
he's away. They send letters and gifts to him in care of his
mother; he, of course, is off skiing in the Alps at the invita-
tion of some other woman who's basking in the pleasure
of his company. Women go crazy for him, they make fools
of themselves to reach him, and they always feel justified
in what they've had to do to get his attention.

Eric doesn't promise marriage or even fidelity. He
doesn't hold out anything much in the way of a future, but
"when he's with you, you feel as if you're the center of his
universe," one woman told me. "He never takes his eyes
off you to look at another woman, no matter how gorgeous
she is. He acts as if you're the most important person in
his life." The truth is, he acts that way with all the women
and they all love him for it.

Leo, a seventy-six-year-old Hollywood writer, has had
at least one beautiful woman either living with him or
wanting to for as long as anyone in town can remember.
He's not a sexual phenomenon and he's not rich. "I don't
give gifts or spend a lot of money on women. I give time
and I do favors. I get their names in the columns and teach
them things like how to read a racing form. Plus I give
them lots of attention. And I'm always supportive. If a
woman says, 'How do I look?' I always say she's beautiful."
If she says, 'I made a mistake,' I say, 'Everyone makes
those mistakes.' "

Right now Leo has a former Miss Texas living with him.

In analyzing men who always have women in love with
them, I looked for regular guys, not extremely handsome,

rich, or powerful ones. I chose men who intuitively pull the right strings with women, men like Henry, the used-car dealer who had a major affair with Liz Taylor.

I admit I was intrigued when I got a chance to interview him in some depth. After all, Liz could have anyone; why choose him? Was he handsome? Not exactly Robert Redford. Was he rich? Hardly. Was he powerful? Not at all. Was he great in bed? Not extraordinarily. But he was sweet and tender, nonjudgmental and accepting. And he had a very seductive hobby. He was a photographer. There's nothing a man can do that is more flattering to a woman than take her picture. It's just about the ultimate way of giving her attention. It appeals to that unfortunate part of a woman's programming which says she's hardly valuable at all unless some man thinks she's beautiful.

Eric, Leo, and Henry all fall into the category of liberated gentlemen, supportive and never demeaning of a woman's abilities, and yet willing to treat her like a queen—opening doors, lighting cigarettes, pulling out her chair. But their true secret is somehow, intuitively, knowing how to create the chemistry of love. "Giving attention" is merely a superficial description of what they do. The way they give their full attention to a woman is the real key.

Creating the Chemistry of Love

True love is built on deep communication, a sense of "oneness" in which you feel totally in tune with each other. You feel that you completely understand and trust each other and that you connect in a way that goes beyond the norm, that's deeper, almost psychic and other-worldly, as if you could read each other's minds in a way that's unique in your experience. You trust each other more than you've ever trusted anyone, and you feel more comfortable together than with anyone else.

If you've ever been deeply and mutually in love with a woman, you've probably experienced this special, deep form of communication. It's a magical feeling, and it's wonderful when it happens as if by magic. But if it's not happening in your life, you can cause it to happen.

What happens when two people are falling in love? They spend time together alone. They gaze into each other's eyes. They act as if they are totally in tune with each other and the rest of the world doesn't exist—they have slipped into that special lovers' communication where they seem to speak without words. What's exciting is that recent discoveries in psychology tell us the process can work in reverse. You can create that special communication with a woman by getting in tune with her love language, and she will feel love.

Love Language

Every person has a primary way of processing the information that he or she is receiving. Just as a child learns best by seeing, hearing, or touching, each of us has a favorite process—a visual, auditory, or feelings process— that he or she is most comfortable with. So, of course, does the woman you love.

The woman you love will decide whether she loves you by what she sees, hears, or feels. By figuring out whether your woman is moved primarily by what she sees, hears, or feels, you'll know the key to winning her love.

When Eric, Leo, and Henry pay total attention to a woman, they also unconsciously slip into her "love language." They intuitively get in tune with her. Flattered by the attention, the woman begins to feel that they are on the same wavelength—a very special feeling—the bonding begins, and the chemistry of love has been created.

Now Eric, Leo, and Henry do this automatically, but if you are willing to devote time to a woman, pay total attention to her when you are with her, and do exactly what I will tell you to do, you can make a woman fall in love just as they do. The steps are simple. By getting in tune with a woman and communicating with her in her love language, she will feel that you understand her better and more deeply than any other man. She'll be driven to see more and more of you. Soon, she'll be hooked—totally, happily in love with you—and you'll be amazed at how easy it all was.

The first step, after being very sure that this is the woman you want, is to find out her love language. When you gaze into her eyes and hang on her every word, you're paying attention to her, but you're also secretly discovering her own special love language.

Once you've discovered whether the woman you want is stimulated more by sights, sounds, or feelings, you will know her love language. Speaking this language and acting in tune with it is the certain path toward being on her wavelength, toward creating the special communication, understanding, and bond that we all recognize as love. Love is still magical when it happens, but now you can have the power to create the magic.

The First Serious Date

You've met a new woman who seems to fit most of your requirements. She's not a witch, bitch, or crazy lady. She has the right look and the right personality. You think you could get serious about her. You're eager to impress her, to make the right moves and say the right words.

You can't help wondering how sexy she is. You fantasize about the two of you going right from lunch to a motel with a dirty movie and a waterbed, or to your apartment. But you don't let fantasies interfere with your mission—to discover her love language.

To set the right tone, remember it's not a good idea to tell her about how some other woman did you wrong or to discuss your past relationships in depth, even if she asks. Especially, don't criticize your ex-wife or ex-girlfriend, thinking it will be obvious how much more you think of the present company. Women don't like it when you criticize your exes because it makes them think you not only have bad manners but bad taste in women as well.

Don't worry about how you're going to impress her with your charm and brilliance and astute judgment. You are going to learn a foolproof method for creating intimacy.

Foolproof Intimacy

Finding out whether your woman is motivated primarily by what she sees, hears, or feels is your first priority. Then you will be able to get on her wavelength and establish intimacy, warmth, and even trust. We all unconsciously trust other people who are like us. By using your woman's love language, you will automatically cause her to start trusting you on a deep unconscious level. Trust is an essential ingredient in any good, lasting relationship.

When you start to relate to a woman in her special love language, she will answer your questions with a new candidness and a feeling that you really understand her. You'll want to ask her questions about herself, to find out about her past relationships and whether she's really available. By being asked the questions in her love language, she'll be more comfortable, and she'll be more inclined to like you right away, trust you, and tell you the truth.

Those first awkward moments when you are alone with a woman, really trying to communicate with her for the first time, will be smoothed over for you when you communicate in her love language. You'll realize the power you've discovered because the conversation will flow smoothly and naturally instead of being guarded and strained. She'll open up to you because she feels comfortable, understood, accepted, and trusting—just because of your choice of words.

Missed Connections

Since everyone—you as well as the woman you are out with—has a visual, auditory, or feelings approach to life, you do have a random chance of matching love languages and hitting it off. On the other hand, chances are twice as great that you won't share the same way of experiencing life and that you could be talking to a woman who's not listening. That's what happens if you speak different languages.

There's nothing worse than being out with a new woman and knowing you're just not making a connection. She starts shredding her napkin, wiggling in her seat, searching through her pocketbook, looking around the room.

Jack, an architect, missed totally on his date with Beth, a therapist. Jack's experience of life came to him through his eyes; he was a totally visual processor of information and ideas. Beth, on the other hand, sensed her world through her feelings. She intuited what was good and bad, what she liked and didn't like, by referring to her inner feelings. The couple decided to have lunch at the beach for their first date. But before they got there, Jack insisted on driving Beth all around the city to see the buildings he had designed. By the time they got to lunch, Beth was eager to sit down someplace quiet and get to know Jack better.

"Let's sit here, where we can see all the action on the beach better," Jack suggested.

"Why don't we sit in the shade, where we'll be more comfortable?" she asked.

"Nah, I'd rather have the view," Jack insisted, sitting in a crowded, not particularly intimate or romantic part of the restaurant's outdoor patio. "So she says okay, and leaves me sitting there while she goes for suntan lotion.

"Then, instead of paying attention to me or listening to me, she spends the whole time with this silly-looking hat on her head, putting suntan stuff on. I was trying to show her a good time at a nice restaurant with a terrific view, and all she worried about was the sun on her face. What a princess. What a disappointment. And I really liked her. I told her how pretty I thought she was."

If Jack had been sensitive to the differences between him and Beth, he would have realized that Beth was a warm, feelings type of woman, just what he said he wanted. Unfortunately, he didn't realize she was sure to be unhappy with him if she felt physically uncomfortable. Had he known, he would have complimented Beth on her nurturing, caring profession instead of her looks. He would have cut down on the strictly visual sightseeing and told her before they got to the restaurant how easy she was to be with, what fun she was, how understanding she was. He would have put his arm around her as he walked her into a place where she would *feel* happy, where they could have a quiet, intimate conversation and be close.

Discovering Her Love Language

By first learning your woman's love language, you will never get into a situation like Jack's, where you do and say all the wrong things hoping to make a woman like you. You'll know precisely the compliments that will make her feel appreciated. She'll know that you see more in her than just another piece of ass. She'll immediately warm up to you because you'll be making the right connections.

You can discover her love language by asking simple, everyday questions and really listening and paying total attention to the answers. Let's say she's just come back from a business trip. It would be natural for you to ask, "How was your trip?"

If she's a visual woman, she might say, "I had a lovely room with a good view, but it never cleared up enough for me to see anything. I never saw the sun one day I was there. The sky was gray the whole time." The woman who experiences her world in an visual way will tell you how things looked.

If she's an auditory woman, she might answer, "Business went well, but my hotel room was so noisy I couldn't sleep. I had a terrible seat on the plane too, right near the engines. It was so noisy I got a headache."

If she's a feelings woman, she'll tell you how the trip felt. "I really felt good about my presentation. I hit my marks and was on a real high. But then afterward, I felt lonely because there was nobody to share my success."

The best kinds of questions to ask are neutral ones, where you don't give clues or "lead the witness." You wouldn't want to say, "How do you feel about your trip?" because you would be asking for a feelings answer. Nor would you want to say, "What did you see on your trip?" Or "What did you hear on your trip?"

You may have to ask several neutral questions before you get a real read on the woman, but you will quickly see a pattern develop. You'll notice that she uses a lot of visual words and describes how things looked to her, or that she talks about what people said to her or what she heard, or that she only tells you how she felt.

As a bonus, you'll notice something else. A lot of your own first-date nervousness will disappear. You have a definite task to perform. You are listening for certain things. You aren't worried so much about whether she likes your tie or whether your breath is fresh enough or whether you're boring her. By asking questions about her, you are getting around most women's biggest objection to a first date. "All the men ever talk about is themselves. They never ask about me. It's just them, them, them. Their job, their kids, their dog, their tennis game, their investments, their car, team, boat, condo."

Good neutral questions are everyday, ordinary questions, the kind people feel comfortable answering. Not "Do you love your parents?" but a light, neutral question, such as "What's your family like?" Ask questions that give your woman room to answer in a visual, auditory, or feelings mode, and to say as little as or as much as she likes.

Here are some examples.

Question: What's your family like?

Visual Answer: They're all blondes like me. My brother's a terrific dresser, but my sister dresses like a hippy, even though she's very pretty.

Auditory Answer: The interesting thing is we all sound alike. Nobody can tell us apart when they hear our voices on the phone. We used to play jokes on people by pretending to be someone else.

Feelings Answer: My parents are really warm and happy and they love each other a lot. We are very touchy; everybody hugs and kisses all the time.

Question: What was your hometown like?

Visual Answer: I was born in an ugly industrial city where the sky was always smoky and everything was dirty and covered with soot. I was so glad to move to a prettier place.

Auditory Answer: It was so quiet where I grew up you could hear a pin drop anywhere in town after ten at night. No loud music, no loud cars, no nothing. Just quiet.

Feelings Answer: I grew up in a small town where everyone knew one another. We were all very close and had a feeling of community. I miss that sometimes.

Question: Tell me about your favorite things to do in your spare time.

Visual Answer: I love to work in the garden. There's something wonderful about seeing a new flower bloom. I could look at my flowers all day.

Auditory Answer: I love to work in my garden because it's so quiet and all you can hear is the birds singing, no phones ringing, no television.

Feelings Answer: I love to work in my garden because I love the way the cool dirt feels between my fingers, and the smell of the grass and flowers.

When you ask the questions, be sure that your tone of voice is one of sincere interest. Don't be flip. Give her your full attention. Lean forward. Let her see by your body language that her answer is important to you.

She'll think you're a wonderful conversationalist and she'll be flattered by your interest. Always follow up with how, why, and where questions. For example, you ask a question and get a short answer.

Question: Where would you live if you could live anywhere?

Answer: The beach.

Question: What do you like about the beach?

Visual Answer: I could just sit on the beach and watch the waves break all day. And I love to watch the sunsets at the beach; they're so beautiful.

Auditory Answer: I love the sound of the waves and the surf breaking and the seagulls squalling.

Feelings Answer: I just love the feeling of being so close to nature, the sand between my toes, the water and sun on my body—it all feels so good. I even like the smell of suntan lotion.

She might even answer, "Oh, I don't know what I like about it, I just like it." Then you should follow up by asking questions in visual, auditory, and feelings languages.

Visual Cue: What are the sunsets like? Do you get a chance to watch them often?

Auditory Cue: I love the roar of the ocean. How does it sound when there's a storm?

Feelings Cue: How does living so close to the ocean affect your moods?

Watch her face very closely. See if she shows more interest when you use visual, auditory, or feelings words. Does her skin color change? Redder means more excitement, more interest. Do her eyes light up? Does she lean forward and seem more excited?

If she just mumbles, "Oh, it's okay I guess," and looks

around and squirms uncomfortably in her seat, you haven't hit on her love language. On the other hand, if she comes alive at your suggestion and begins to talk animatedly, you may have the key to her inner responses.

Once you begin to get a clue whether your woman is visual, auditory, or feelings, then follow up to be certain. Check and double-check her responses. Try other questions. Confirm her pattern.

Don't worry if you feel uncomfortable asking all the questions, not talking about yourself, just listening. It's okay and she'll love it. The more you can get her to talk, the more comfortable she'll feel with you. If she asks why you're asking so many questions, say something like "Well, I'm really interested in you."

After the first date, you will have a good idea of the type of woman you have and how to talk to her in her love language. You'll know that if you want to see her again, she'll want to see you. A man who really listens, who knows how to communicate in a woman's love language, is an alchemist who can create the chemistry of love whenever he wants. The next three chapters explain each type of woman and tell exactly what to do to make her yours.

CHAPTER SIX

The Visual Woman

Your visual woman lives in a world of images. Appearance is important to her. Although her hearing is fine and she has feelings like everyone else, her wavelength is visual. If you take her to a wonderful concert, she may or may not remember the beautiful music, but she'll definitely have a mental picture of the stage and the orchestra and what you both wore that evening.

You spot a visual woman right away by her good fashion sense. She's always well dressed, no matter what the situation. She may dress trendily, or she may have her own special style. Whatever she wears, it looks right on her. Her shoes are shined, and she wouldn't be caught dead with chipped nail polish.

She'll roll up your sleeves, turn up your collar, adjust your outfit, and help you look perfectly turned out for any occasion. If you let her, she'll be happy to take you shopping and pick out all your clothes. Actually, the first sign that a visual woman is in love is that she starts redecorating the love object, you.

Your visual woman's apartment seems to have been put together by a decorator's touch. She has a keen sense of color and design. She can turn almost anything into a decorative household accessory, even without spending a lot of money. In her hands, a few fans from Chinatown become a fabulous wall display; some old photographs arranged on a table look like something out of a decorating magazine. Since she loves having bouquets of fresh flowers around, you can never go wrong bringing her a bunch.

Everywhere she goes, heads turn, not because she is necessarily so gorgeous but because she makes the best of what she has. She always looks terrific. If she's cleaning, she ties a scarf around her head and winds up looking like Carmen Miranda with a broom. If she's hiking, she looks like she just walked out of an L. L. Bean catalog. She looks good scrubbing floors, digging in the garden, even getting up in the morning.

The way to a visual woman's heart is to dress the way she likes, look at her adoringly and lovingly, and let her see your love. The danger is that you can be totally taken in by how good she looks and never stop to find out about the person under the looks.

The Visual Personality

The visual woman is usually a Type A.—quick-moving, never sitting still for very long, always doing something. That's because she absorbs information primarily with her eyes and she wants to move around to see as much as possible.

The visual woman is very organized. Given half a chance, she will organize your life, just like hers, into neat and tidy compartments. She becomes visibly upset when things are out of place and messy. Some people think she's rigid and inflexible just because she likes everything to be in perfect order.

She prefers face-to-face conversations to telephone messages, but her favorite means of communication is a picture or letter, or even a meaningful glance or expression.

She prefers analyzing how things look to her, not how they sound or feel. A visual women sometimes doesn't seem as warm as other women because she has trouble letting it all hang out emotionally. She's more controlled, more emotionally conforming. Sometimes you may need to help a visual woman express her feelings, either by expressing yours or by giving suggestions and asking questions.

Talking about love can be wasted on the visual woman; she needs to see how much you love her. You can show this by writing her a note, leaving her a small trinket, or giving her flowers or a picture of the two of you together.

Visual Eyes

Throughout the world, in every language or society, a man or woman's eye movements mirror his or her inner thoughts. The person's age or life experience doesn't matter. His or her eye movements will tell you more than their words.

Gazing into a woman's eyes is sexy, romantic, and exciting to her. Actually, she doesn't know it but her eyes are giving her away. By learning to read her small but easily observable eye movements, you'll learn something about her that she herself doesn't know—her love language.

No matter what she says to you, her eyes will always reveal the truth. As you learn to read them, you will be able to look into her thoughts and actually read her mind. You'll be able to "watch" her decision-making process, and you'll be able to get her to decide in your favor. You'll be able to reach her soul in a way nobody else can.

Everyone, of course, looks up once in a while. Most people, even if they're not visual, will tend to look up when they're being asked to visualize. Visual people, on the other hand, look up a lot—whenever they're remembering or imagining.

When you ask the question "What was your school like?" the visualizing woman will answer with a visual description. "It was an old-fashioned school, with brick buildings covered in green ivy. It looked like a picture postcard." While she's remembering, her eyes will look up and to one side or the other.

At first, you may not be sure about your woman's eye movements. Your ability to read them will improve with practice. Keep asking questions until you're sure you've detected a definite pattern. If her eye movements are upward and she's answering with visual descriptions, you can be sure her love language is visual.

Keep the questions neutral. Never ask, "What did your school look like?" because then she could be responding visually simply because you gave her a visual cue.

Visualizers tend to look up and to one side when remembering something they saw in their past, and up and to the other side when imagining something they've never seen before. Once you figure out this pattern, you'll really be able to read your woman's mind.

A corporate attorney came to me for help because he was having problems with the woman he loved. He was very upset because he felt distanced from her. "We don't seem to be able to communicate. Whenever I want to talk to her, I feel like she's on another planet. I tell her I love her, but she doesn't seem to be impressed.

I even told her I thought we'd be able to form a serious relationship, and she didn't react at all. I couldn't believe my ears. There I was practically proposing and she says, 'Do you see anything on the menu that looks good to you?' "

It was immediately obvious that my auditory client had a visual woman. As soon as I explained to him why he wasn't getting anywhere, he was able to change his strategy. Being a lawyer, he had always assumed that a correctly worded statement assured effective communication. He learned that the woman he loved simply operated on a different wavelength. If she was visually distracted, she would totally block out auditory inputs. So he started making sure that she was looking at him before he initiated any serious conversation. Whenever there was anything really important to communicate, he talked to her using visual words and then reinforced his conversation by leaving her little notes, signed with a silly, happy face. She loved finding his notes and cherished every word. His next proposal was accepted immediately.

Visual Tests

QUESTIONS TO FIND OUT IF SHE'S A VISUAL WOMAN

(Watch her eye movements and listen to her answers. Check for visual words and upward eye movements.)

What was your childhood like?
What did you like about your first boyfriend?
What's the best part of your job?
What's the worst part of your job?

QUESTIONS TO INVOKE A PAST VISUAL MEMORY

What was your hometown like?
Do you remember your grandmother?
Who was your favorite President?
What was your first job like?

QUESTIONS TO INVOKE AN IMAGINARY IMAGE

Would you like to go in a spaceship?
What would you like to be doing in five years?
What would it be like to be a rock star?
What would you do if you won the lottery?

Although most visual women will have a consistent up-to-the-right or up-to-the-left eye pattern, a few may not. Occasionally, a visualizer will just stare straight ahead with a glassy-eyed, fixed stare and dilated pupils. If you ask your lady enough questions and pay total attention to her, her particular pattern will become unmistakable to you.

Another test to find out if you have a visual woman is to check out her breathing. Visual women tend to breathe rapidly, high in their chests, as opposed to breathing deeply and slowly.

In order to find out what your visual woman is thinking, follow up on her eye movements, even if she hasn't said a word. Ask her, "How do you picture that?" Or, "What do you see?" Or, "Can you see what I mean?"

For instance, ask her, "Would you like to go to a movie tonight?" If she looks up to her past visual side, you can guess that she's thinking of a movie she's seen before, or even remembering an ad for a movie she'd like to see. You might follow up with "Have you seen any good movies advertised?" If she looks up and to her future visual side, you might ask, "What movie would you like to see?"

She'll feel so deeply understood that she'll answer exactly what she was thinking. She might say, "That's amazing that you should mention an ad. I was thinking of one I saw in today's paper." She'll feel as if you and she have a very special connection, as if you can read her mind.

When you discover your woman's eye movements as she visualizes something from her past, or sees something in her imagination she's never seen before, write them down. Use the chart on the next page. All you have to do is fill in the eyes.

How to Talk to the Visual Woman

When you're talking to the visual woman, keep in mind that you are not on her favorite wavelength. You may think she's listening, while in fact she's actually preoccupied with a mental picture of something—a vacation spot, a new dress, or a problem from her job.

She may seem a bit spacey at times, but you can get through to her just fine if you express your thoughts in visual words. She'll get the picture right away.

"The three Rs": A *R*ight-handed woman *R*emembers a visual image on your *R*ight as you face her.

A *right*-handed woman *creates* a visual image on your left as you face her.

A *left*-handed woman *remembers* a visual image on your left as you face her.

A *left*-handed woman *creates* a visual image on your right as you face her.

Your woman. (Fill in)

What the Visual Woman Is Likely to Say to You

(The visual cue words are in italic.)

You *look* great tonight.
I have a new *perspective* on our relationship.
Do you *see* what I mean?
Do you *see* how I feel?
Do you *see* what I'm talking about?
I can *see* what you're saying and it makes sense to me.
I have a *clearer picture* now.
I love to *watch* people.
I can *see* two sides to that argument.
I could *see* a destructive *pattern* with my ex.
I can *picture* you driving a *bright red* truck.
After I *looked* at my past relationships, my mistakes be-
    came *clear*.
I've *drawn a blank*.
From my *point of view*, this *looks* perfect.

When you answer your visual woman, you should use
picture words and visual images. Here are some words
that will get your visual woman's attention.

What You Should Say to the Visual Woman

(The visual cue words are in italic.)

I'm beginning to *see* the *light*.
It's *clear* to me now.
I love to *look* at you.
I can *picture* us together.
Seeing you makes me *light* up.
You *look* beautiful in the *moonlight*.

I want a *picture* of you.
Your eyes *shine* like *bright* stars.
We *look* good together.
That *color* makes your complexion *radiate*.
It's *clear* to me that we should *look* at this again.
I'm a little *foggy* on that. Maybe you can *clear* it up.
Let's get this into *focus*.
I'll never *look* at another woman.

If you care more about how things sound or feel, using visual words may seem uncomfortable at first. It may seem awkward for you to use unfamiliar expressions, but this visual mode will sound natural to her. She's the one who'll be listening and hearing the words that make a clear picture for her. She'll be delighted to have found someone with whom she can really communicate.

Remember that these are clear, valid, common words. You can express your thoughts just as honestly with visual words as with any other words. And the effort spent learning to communicate visually won't be wasted even if you decide you don't like the woman. You can use this technique on any other visual person with whom it is important for you to communicate. Being able to change gears linguistically makes you a more powerful person.

If the woman you want is visual, simply changing the words you use is the first step toward winning her. Soon it will be natural for you to use visual expressions with her. The more you think visually, the more you will convince the visual woman that you really understand and appreciate her. Because you are speaking her language, she'll unconsciously want to agree with what you say.

So if you usually say, "I understand how you feel" or "I hear you," try saying, "I can see how you feel." It may sound strange to you, but it will sound perfectly natural to her. If you usually say, "That doesn't sound right to me," try saying, "That doesn't look right to me."

Visual words are her love language. Using them will help you avoid misunderstandings and make her feel understood. She'll be closer, more intimate, and more in tune with you. You will have a growing power of persuasion over her.

How the Visual Woman Spends Her Time

Window-shopping
Watching television or going to the movies
People-watching
Decorating her house
Going to art exhibits and museums
Taking long drives on the scenic route
Reading
Going to the theater
Looking at you
Looking in mirrors, combing her hair, checking her
    makeup
Putting on makeup
Putting outfits together
Watching sunsets

What the Visual Woman Does for a Living

Filmmaker
Eye doctor
Makeup artist
Photographer
Decorator
Artist
Designer
Graphic artist

Computer graphics operator
Clothes saleswoman
Media consultant
Museum staff member

How to Make Love to the Visual Woman

√ First of all, if you're a slob, this is the woman to clean your house for. If you can't, hire a maid before she comes. There is nothing more certain to make a visual woman uncomfortable than disorder. If your place is beyond hope, try going to her place until you get yours fixed up. Do *not* try to make love to the visual woman surrounded by your piles of dirty underwear and old beer bottles.

√ Dress for her. No old torn clothes, no socks with holes, no shoes with rundown heels, and no shirts with frayed cuffs or collars. Your visual woman will notice everything, and you'll lose points with her if you show up looking grubby.

If you don't know what to wear, go to a chic men's store and have them dress you for the occasion. Or ask her. She loves to tell people what to wear. If you clean up your apartment, you could even let her come over and pick out your clothes. Or let her take you shopping. She loves to be visually creative and wouldn't mind helping you look chic.

√ Also, wear what she thinks is sexy. If she says she likes red bikini briefs and you like boxer shorts, this is a good chance to show your flexibility and make easy points with her. If she buys you something or goes shopping with you and helps you pick it out, wear it, use it, display it. She will definitely notice if you don't.

√ Smile at her a lot. It's a visual way to let her know you're happy with her. Take her picture or pictures of the two of you together and give them to her.

The visual woman is even more susceptible than most women to being visually appreciated. She likes you to ✓ notice and compliment her on the way she looks. Let her know you appreciate her. And never, ever tell her anything looks less than perfect on her.

The visual woman likes her lovemaking preceded by lots of visual courting. Courting is old-fashioned romance. It means you spend time together doing things that build pleasure and expectation, closeness and intimacy. For the visual woman, that means taking her someplace with a nice view—a walk on the beach, an art show, a waterfront or high-rise restaurant. Courting the visual woman means ✓ looking at her a lot and letting her look at you.

Talking too much about your feelings too soon can be a turnoff for a visual woman. She is slow to express her feelings and wants to see that everything looks right before she commits herself. Communicate your feelings to her gradually, not in a gush of emotion—a sure way to make her back off.

Your time spent making everything look good for her will be appreciated. Your visual woman actually gets excited by what she sees. Yes, if something looks good to her, ✓ she gets sexually aroused. Just as some women are aroused by the sound of Ravel's "Bolero" or the feel of mink, she's turned on by the look of something that's visually pleasing.

To find out what she likes in the way of visual stimulation, look at her and her apartment. Check out the style, the colors. She is a mirror of what she likes.

Make sure your bedroom is attractively decorated, and set it up to be visually stimulating. Bring out your (tasteful!) erotic art. If you have a picture of your ex, put it away. Set up flattering soft lighting, hang nice art, put color-coordinated towels in the bathroom. Put decorator linens on the bed. Cover the metal bed frame if it shows. Nothing turns her off more than an ugly bed.

Ask her if she likes the decor. If she objects to something—say, a photograph you've always thought was very sexy—remove it. Being visually pleased turns her on. Being visually disturbed makes her want to leave. So let her have her way with the visuals; you can choose the music.

Have a freshly washed and neatly pressed linen hand towel by the bed for afterward. Break out a brand-new tube of KY. Have fresh soap in the bathroom. She'll definitely notice and be turned off by anything scuzzy.

A visual woman who came to one of my workshops was having a lot of trouble finding the right man. It seemed that the men she really liked were feelings men, but she couldn't resist trying to redo them so that they fit her preconceived visual ideas of how the man she was with should look. When they came over to her house, she would constantly bustle around, cooking and cleaning up—a minor whirlwind who made the feelings men uncomfortable and drove them away.

"I'm almost afraid to go out with the new man in my life, he dresses so badly," she told the group. "I mean, I never know what he's going to show up wearing and I'm really afraid he'll embarrass me." Naturally, that relationship didn't work out for her either. Then she met a man who absolutely had her number. He knew exactly how to make love to her, so that she fell madly in love with him after just one evening. Later, she told me about it.

"He invited me to his place, high in the hills above Sunset Boulevard. When I got there, he didn't do what lots of guys do. There was no grabbing and groping. He barely kissed my cheek, and invited me to have a seat with him on the balcony. We sat on either side of a small table where we could see each other, and we drank champagne and watched the sunset and then the lights twinkling in the dark.

"Inside, he had the most beautiful mood lighting that made everything glow just a little. By then, he had barely touched me physically, but his eyes were beginning to look into my soul as no other man has.

"We ate dinner by candlelight, watching the constantly moving stream of car lights below, and then looking into each other's eyes as we talked. After dinner, he showed me his art collection, which included a couple of very erotic but tasteful prints. I began to get turned on by the way he looked at the art, tenderly, lovingly.

"I could tell by the way he looked at me that he thought I was very sexy and attractive. He didn't have to say a word. Slowly, he began touching me, like an artist admiring a statue; he began to study first my shoulders, then, as he unbuttoned my blouse, each part of my body almost inch by inch, touching, admiring me, almost wordlessly. Just the way he looked at my breast made me want him.

"Instead of just throwing my good silk blouse aside, he hung it up carefully, smoothing it out. Watching him touch the silk blouse so gently and sensuously made me yearn to have him touch me the same way. By the time we hit the bedroom, I was more turned on than I ever remember, just from watching him watching me.

"He told me how beautiful he thought I was, admiring each part of my body—my hair, my lips, my eyes—kissing me all over, but first looking at each part as if he was examining a fine work of art.

"We've been on several dates, and each time it's a visual feast. Sometimes we rent sexy movies and stay home. I've never been so in love before."

Remember, your visual woman wants to get a good look at what she's going to get before she gets it. She doesn't like being grabbed and thrown down. Don't rush up and hug her or press for too much physical closeness until she's had a chance to look at you for a while. Looking makes her desires flame.

What You Are

Visual Man. If you are very neat, if the things in your closet and on your dresser are lined up in rows, if you are more of a Type A personality—high-strung, workaholic, foot-jiggling, always moving around—you are probably a visual man. You prefer looking at a map to hearing directions told to you. You prefer to see something first, and will decide if you like it based on whether it looks good to you or not.

Visual Man/Visual Woman. You may think you're the perfect match, but unfortunately, you may not be. You may see things differently, or be both very visually set in your ways and unwilling to change. She likes country, you're set on modern. Two visual people can find it harder to make the visual compromises necessary to live together. Also, you may be choosing each other on looks alone, which isn't the best basis for a long-lasting relationship.

Auditory Man. You could well be an engineer or a high-tech type. That's because your mind is so organized. You are a logical thinker. Not exactly a fashion plate, you prefer casual clothes to dressy ones. You are not known for neatness and your sense of style. You are a good talker and listener and decide things based on how they sound.

Auditory Man/Visual Woman. You will have to straighten up and dress up for the visual woman, and remember to notice how she looks. Since how things look is not as important to you as it is to her, you'll have to be willing to let her decorate the way she wants. You may be disappointed with her sometimes because she doesn't say the words you need to hear. You'll have to tell her what you want her to say, just as she'll have to tell you what she wants you to wear. On the positive side, she'll bring visual pleasures and stimulation into your life and you'll bring auditory pleasures into hers.

Feelings Man. You are the most sensitive and the most in touch with your feelings of all men. You are mellower, slower-moving, and would rather be comfortable than anything else. You like to touch a lot and make your decisions based on how things feel. Your emotions are close to the surface. You love eating and sleeping and soft skin and your favorite chair.

Feelings Man/Visual Woman. Since the visual woman is so turned on or off by what she sees, you'll have to be really careful about your very, very casual sense of fashion and decor. Eating is more important to you than it is to her. She'd rather have less food that doesn't taste as good but is served beautifully in a nice setting. Be sure to compliment her on her looks, and don't scare her off with too many feelings too soon.

The Auditory Woman

Your auditory woman cares most about sounds. How you sound, the pitch and tone of your voice, and the words you use are what's most important to her. Although there's nothing wrong with her eyes, she may not notice what may seem obvious to you. Her feelings are also intact, but they are not her first point of reference. The auditory woman will always relate better to music than to pictures, to the inner logic of words than to feelings.

The auditory woman is easy to communicate with because she enjoys conversation. She talks to you and she talks to herself. Sometimes she may seem distant only because she's busy having a conversation with herself.

The way to an auditory woman's heart is to be a good listener, to really hear what she has to say, and to communicate verbally as much as possible. She finds nonverbal communication boring and confusing.

Your auditory woman is extremely logical, and she remembers what she hears better than others do. So be careful what you say to her; she won't forget. She'll listen carefully, not only to what you say but also to what you don't say. Change your usual greeting and she'll be suspicious. She will notice inconsistencies in your stories. Never try to hide something from her on the phone. All she has to do is hear you say hello and she knows whether you're happy or sad, relaxed or anxious, hiding something or open.

The Auditory Personality

An auditory woman tends to be more easygoing and relaxed than a visual woman. She doesn't have to see something to understand it, so she just sits still and listens.

Her favorite activities are passive: reading, working on creative projects, listening to music, and talking. She's a cerebral type who lives in her mind. Although she's always doing something, it usually isn't hustling and bustling around. Often she'll be just as content to hear about something as to go and see it for herself.

She prefers in-person or telephone conversations to writing letters or memos. As soon as she gets in the car, she turns on the radio. When she comes in the house, she turns on the stereo or the television. She loves the sound of voices.

She is quick to let you hear about it if she's angry or upset. She's articulate and expresses herself well. She loves discussing issues, is knowledgeable, and enjoys telling people what she knows. Sometimes when you tell her about a problem she may seem unsympathetic because she tends to start analyzing the problem instead of giving you the hug you really want. If you need sympathy, you may just have to tell her you want it. Thank her for her advice, but say, "I hear what you're saying and those all sound like good ideas, but right now what sounds best is a hug."

There are two types of auditory women. One is always filling the silences in one way or another. The other is very sensitive to any sound at all and prefers complete silence. Any sound is an interruption of the conversation she's having with herself, particularly if it's not a sound she's chosen. Both types of auditory women can be stimulated to have loving feelings toward you by the words you say and the tone of voice you say them in.

If you want her to remember something, just tell her. You don't have to show her, leave notes, or draw maps. She'd prefer that you just tell her anyway.

She talks on the phone a lot, but tends to resent it when you have long intimate conversations with others. It's almost as if you're giving them something that's hers. Because she's such a good conversationalist, she can be the life of the party when she gets started. She's more flexible than the visual woman because she doesn't care so much how things look.

Although she's very good at organizing her thoughts in a logical order, her belongings seem to get away from her. She can be somewhat untidy, because whenever she begins organizing her things, she starts to have long conversations with herself about where they should go and about all the future ramifications of her choice. So if you're expecting perfection in housekeeping, you won't find it with an auditory woman.

The best way to let an auditory woman know you love her is to tell her over and over again as often as you possibly can. If you don't have a pet name for her, think of one.

Sometimes she gets upset for no reason. Everything seems fine and then she's ready to fight. That's because she's been having a discussion in her head about an issue—perhaps for days—before she lets you in on it.

She hates screaming and yelling, especially if you do it.

You can say almost anything to her as long as you keep your tone pleasant.

Auditory Eyes

Watch your woman's eyes to confirm whether she's auditory or not. By watching closely you can look into her mind. The auditory woman's eyes almost always dart to one side when she's thinking, or when she's having a conversation with herself, or when she's evaluating what you've just said. Once in a while she looks up, because she can visualize as well, but mostly she looks toward her ears.

It's important not to mix up a visual woman and an auditory woman. The auditory woman has likes and needs that are definitely different from those of the visual woman. When you ask a woman out or plan a date, it's very, very important to know if she's a visual, auditory, or feelings woman. If you are visual, as many men tend to be, you may be tempted to plan an entirely visual date for a woman who won't appreciate it.

A man who came to me for relationship counseling was having trouble with a woman he was in love with. "I know she likes me, but I can't seem to figure out what to do or where to go when we're together. I took her to a friend's art opening and she seemed bored. I wanted to show her this particular exhibit, and she glanced at it and that was all. It meant nothing to her.

"I took her out to the wine country for the weekend. In autumn, when the colors are changing, it's very beautiful. We tasted wines and had a picnic one afternoon, but I could tell she was restless. She complained because the stereo in my car wasn't working. She was bored. Do you think we're just incompatible? I mean, we get along great in bed and I really like her, but I'm worried that we'll never find anything we like to do together."

Since he had already tried visual experiences (beautiful scenery) and feelings experiences (picnics and wine tasting) and she hadn't responded, he needed to try an auditory experience, like a concert or a lecture. He reported that on their next date, a concert, she was a lot more enthusiastic.

Obviously, he had been dating an auditory woman and providing her with visual experiences. By learning to think in an auditory way, he was able to begin a whole new relationship with the woman he cared about.

"Now we spend lots of time talking. She says I'm rare and wonderful because I really listen and seem to hear what she says."

He noticed, too, that when he asked her questions, she answered by telling how things sounded. For example, he asked her where she grew up. She said it was in a noisy industrial city where you could hardly hear yourself think. Also, her eyes looked toward the side, a definitely auditory sign.

By asking lots of questions and watching your auditory woman's eye movements, you'll be able to figure out where she looks when she's remembering a sound from the past and where she looks when she's imagining a sound she's never heard before.

When Brett and Darlene came to me, they had been dating for some time, but Brett felt that Darlene wasn't affectionate enough. Brett was a feelings man, and he needed to touch and be touched a lot. He thought Darlene looked away too much, and was bothered by her looking away when he touched her. Darlene, an auditory woman, didn't care for his nonverbal, touching communication style; she needed to be told she was loved.

Brett learned not to walk in a room and just grab Darlene without saying something first. As long as he kept talking, Darlene didn't mind his touching at all. She understood what each touch meant.

"I love the nape of your neck," he told her, touching it gently. "I love the way you taste," he told her, kissing her. Slowly, talking all the while, he found that he was able to make their lovemaking much more exciting and that she was more responsive than she'd ever been before. Soon Darlene began telling Brett that she liked parts of his body and touching him back. They are still together.

You can tell if your woman is auditory by using your senses. Watch her eyes. Listen to the words she uses. Test her responses to pictures, to sounds, to feelings. The auditory woman always responds best to sounds.

Auditory Tests

QUESTIONS TO FIND OUT IF SHE'S AN AUDITORY WOMAN

(Watch her eye movements and listen to the answers. Check for auditory words and side-to-side eye movements.)

What was your childhood like?
What did you like about your first boyfriend?
What do you like about your job?
What's the worst part of your job?

QUESTIONS TO INVOKE A PAST AUDITORY MEMORY

(Watch her look to one side when she answers. That's where she'll always look when remembering something she's heard before.)

What's your favorite music?
Do you ever hear your mother's voice in your mind?

Did you grow up in a quiet town?
What did you tell yourself about tonight?

QUESTIONS TO INVOKE AN IMAGINARY AUDITORY
    RESPONSE

(When she answers, she'll look to the side opposite her
past memory side. That's where she'll always look when
she imagines hearing something.)

What would you sound like if you were a man?
How would you sound if you were an opera singer?
If you were a deaf person, would you try to speak or learn
    sign language?

How to Talk to the Auditory Woman

Speak up when you're talking to your auditory woman.
She's not impressed by a knowing nod. Don't depend on
a loving gaze to communicate your feelings; tell her.
Don't just listen when she's talking; make little sounds
every once in a while so she knows you're listening. Practice using auditory words so that you really get her attention. To her, auditory words are like hearing her own
name across a crowded room.

What the Auditory Woman Is Likely to Say to You

(The auditory words are in italic.)

Just *listening* to you makes me feel better.
That *sounds* like a good idea.

Let's sit *quietly* and *talk* things over.
A little *voice tells* me you're not *telling* the truth.
Did you *hear* what I *said*.
I can *tune in* or *tune out* when I want.
Your *voice* always *sounds* sexy to me.
Harmony is important to me.
I *heard* it *clear as a bell*.
My ex gave me a lot of *static*.
That has a negative *ring* to it.
Why don't we *listen* to some *music?*
Everything's *clicking* into place.
It *sounds* like you didn't *hear* what I *said*.

When you answer your auditory woman, you should use
auditory words. Here are some words that will get your
auditory woman's attention.

What You Should Say to the Auditory Woman

(The auditory words are in italic.)

I *hear* you *clear as a bell*.
Let's *talk* about how we can get more *in tune*.
The *sound* of your *voice* is *music* to my *ears*.
Something *tells* me we're right for each other.
I have this idea about us *rattling* around in my head.
What you *said rings a bell* with me.
I love to *hear the sound of your voice*.
That *sounds* like a good idea.
You *sound* like you want to *talk*.
I'd like to *discuss* this *quietly*, without *shouting*.
If you could *hear* yourself, you wouldn't *say* that.
I want us to be on the same *frequency*.
If you *tell* me what's on your mind, I'll be your *sounding*
    board.

It's not what you *said*, it's your *tone of voice* that bothers me.

If you care more about how things look or feel, using auditory words may seem uncomfortable at first. It may seem awkward for you to use unfamiliar expressions, but this auditory mode will sound natural to her. She's the one who'll be listening and hearing the words that make music for her. Your auditory expressions will sound natural to her. She'll be delighted to have found someone with whom she can really communicate.

Remember that these are clear, valid, common words. You can express your thoughts just as honestly with auditory words as with any other words. And the effort spent learning to communicate auditorily won't be wasted even if you decide you don't like the woman. You can use this technique on any other auditory person with whom it is important for you to communicate. Being able to change gears linguistically makes you a more powerful person.

If the woman you want is auditory, simply changing the words you use is the first step toward winning her. Soon it will be natural for you to use auditory expressions with her. The more you think auditorily, the more you will convince the auditory woman that you really understand and appreciate her. Because you are speaking her language, she'll unconsciously want to agree with what you say.

So if you usually say, "I understand how you feel" or "I see what you mean," try saying, "I hear you." It may sound strange to you, but it will sound perfectly natural to her. If you usually say, "That doesn't look right to me," try saying, "That doesn't sound right to me."

Auditory words are her love language. Using them will help you avoid misunderstandings and make her feel understood. She'll be closer, more intimate, and more in tune with you. You will have a growing power of persuasion over her.

How the Auditory Woman Spends Her Time

Listening to her stereo or going to concerts
Talking on the telephone
Playing a musical instrument
Dancing
Listening to tapes of lectures or books
Leaving the television on, but not necessarily watching
Writing scripts in her head for future conversations
Replaying past conversations in her head, wondering if
  she said the right thing, or what someone meant, or
  what she could have said instead of what she did say
Eavesdropping on other people's conversations
Having long heart-to-heart conversations with friends
Listening to the radio
Enjoying the sounds of nature, the ocean, and the birds

What the Auditory Woman Does for a Living

Telephone saleswoman
Teacher
Works in radio
Works in the music business
Therapist or counselor
Singer
Musician
Lawyer
Public relations person
Writer
Editor
Publisher

How to Make Love to the Auditory Woman

When your auditory woman is coming over to spend the
night, stack the records on the stereo and turn the music
on before you worry about cleaning up your place. She'll
be more impressed if the music sounds right to her than
if the place looks neat. She buys the best in stereo, and
good sound is important to her.

She loves the sounds of lovemaking. If you can muster
up a noisy orgasm, she'll be really impressed. If you just
quietly come, she'll think you're not enjoying yourself.
Let her know that you enjoy her.

This means lots of talk before, during, and after. You
court the auditory woman by talking, not by kissing.
Spend a lot of time telling her how much you appreciate
her. Let her know you're her biggest fan and she'll be a
pushover for you.

Never just grab her and throw her down, or even rush
up to touch her. She needs to talk first. Talk turns her on.
Talk gets her in the mood for love. If you're the strong
silent type, you won't last long with an auditory woman.

For foreplay, the auditory woman needs talk. Talk is her
aphrodisiac, her biggest turn-on. A long heart-to-heart,
soul-to-soul conversation will mean more to her than the
greatest sexual performance, and even a mediocre performance is a symphony for her if it's accompanied by the
right words.

The auditory woman's pace is mellow, not hurried. She
doesn't like rushed lovemaking. You need to spend time
with her, and slowly the two of you drift toward the bedroom—naturally, as if you are drawn there.

Notice how she breathes, slowly, regularly, deeply from
the diaphragm rather than high up in the chest. Notice
how the tone of her voice is regulated, not too high, not
too low. Notice how she paces her conversation almost as
if she were speaking in time to a silent metronome that

only she can hear. This is the pace you should try to emulate when you're making love with the auditory woman.

She may not notice the flowers in the vase, or the new
pictures on the wall, but you can be sure she'll notice
whether you're in tune with her or not.

Although the auditory woman loves a good discussion,
never, ever raise your voice. Make love to her with the
music of your voice and the words you say. She loves
poetry and sexy stories. Find a great erotic tale to read
aloud to her; she'll love it.

Then, slowly, reading or talking all the time, touch her,
exploring her body as you talk. She's pretty easy to make
happy—all you have to do is say the right words. If you're
good at talking dirty, your auditory woman can be turned
on just by erotic words. Before you get to the bedroom,
talk to her about what you're going to do and how you're
going to make love to her. Just telling her what you're
going to do will make her feel sexually excited. With the
proper verbal foreplay, she'll be ready and waiting for you
to make love.

Play the same music she plays at home. That way she'll
feel relaxed. Match your vocal tone to hers. Talk to her
about the sounds of love. Tell her, "Your voice turns me
on." Or, "Our bodies seem to be perfectly in tune with
each other."

Say her name a lot, especially during lovemaking. It will
reassure her that you know who you're with and that you
think she's special. You can go down on her until your
tongue falls off, you can be the greatest lover ever, but if
you don't talk to your auditory woman, you'll lose her to
someone who does. She is turned off by a man who doesn't
express himself verbally. She thinks you're withholding,
even if you think you have nothing to say.

One auditory woman told me she was madly in love
with a man after the first time they made love. He had
given her the ultimate auditory experience. "It was the

most exciting night of my life. First we went to dinner and we talked and talked, and then we went to his place and we talked and talked until three in the morning, and then we went to bed. We talked in bed for about another hour, and while we were talking, he began touching me all over. By the time we made love, I was more turned on than I ever remember.

"And he talked while we made love, telling me how beautiful I was and how good I felt and how much he was enjoying being with me. Then, when I touched him, he groaned with pleasure. That sound made me an animal. I couldn't keep my hands off his body. And when I touched him with my mouth, he kept saying, 'Oh God, oh God, I've never felt like this before,' and that spurred me on to more.

"Then we became like a vocal rendition of dueling guitars, the sounds he made spurring me on and the sounds I made spurring him on. At the end, we were both making these incredible, primitive, passionate animal sounds that took us into another consciousness. I could hear myself screaming with pleasure, and he was yelling, 'Come with me, come with me! Oh God, I'm coming, I'm coming!' and then there were just the sounds of our two orgasms. I don't think I'll be able to live without making love to him again. We were a concerto of male and female orgasms. I'll never forget that sound."

What You Are

Visual Man. If you are very neat, if the things in your closet and on your dresser are lined up in rows, if you are more of a Type A personality—high-strung, workaholic, foot-jiggling, always moving around—you are probably an auditory man. You prefer looking at a map to hearing directions told to you. You prefer to see something first and will decide if you like it based on whether it looks good to you or not.

Visual Man/Auditory Woman. If you're a visual man, you might become frustrated by your auditory woman's lack of interest in making her surroundings visually pleasing. You may become upset because she doesn't notice that you've shaved off your mustache, but don't worry. It's an asset to have a woman who's more interested in the inner you, who appreciates that you look good but doesn't make good looks the most important thing in her life. Listen to her. You may find you like what you hear enough to make up for what she doesn't notice.

Auditory Man. You could well be an engineer or a high-tech type. That's because your mind is so organized. You are a logical thinker. Not exactly a fashion plate, you prefer casual clothes to dressy ones. You are not known for neatness and your sense of style. You are a good talker and listener and decide things based on how they sound.

Auditory Man/Auditory Woman. If you're an auditory man and you're interested in an auditory woman, you should have no trouble at all. You will hear each other loud and clear, and with very little trouble you'll be able to ring her bell. The two of you can enjoy long hours talking on the phone, discussing philosophy and the universe, or sharing music and concerts.

Feelings Man. You are the most sensitive and the most in touch with your feelings of all men. You are mellower, slower-moving, and would rather be comfortable than anything else. You like to touch a lot and make your decisions based on how things feel. Your emotions are close to the surface. You love eating and sleeping and soft skin and your favorite chair.

Feelings Man/Auditory Woman. If you're a feelings man, be sure to talk to the auditory woman while you're touching her. Don't try to communicate nonverbally with her and never assume that she understands how you feel. She's a woman to whom you have to tell your feelings. Happy or hurt, she needs to hear it to believe it.

CHAPTER EIGHT

The Feelings Woman

Your feelings woman is the most sensitive and most easily hurt of all women. She is also the easiest to please. She is the most intuitive, the most understanding, and the most simpatico of women as well. She will rely on how she feels when you're together rather than on how cute you are or whether you wear the right clothes or drive the right car or say the right words.

A feelings woman is easy to get close to because she is so open and emotional. She is quick to trust her instinct and knows when a relationship feels right to her.

Your feelings woman is easy to communicate with because she doesn't need words or pictures, she gets the message by sensing it. She doesn't have the steel-trap computer mind of the auditory woman or the observant eye of the visual woman, so she may not notice at first if you lie to her, but she will sense that something is wrong.

The way to your feelings woman's heart is to exhibit your own feelings freely and easily. Tell her how you feel, touch her a lot, express your vulnerability, cry at movies, show compassion and sympathy for others. These things impress her most.

The Feelings Personality

The feelings woman is the most giving woman of all. She gives to everyone, sometimes to extremes. She's the type who picks up stray people just so she can help them. She may also take in stray or hurt animals and is a sure sale for any door-to-door salesman with a heartrending story.

She can't contain her feelings. If she's happy, she's ecstatic. If she's sad, she's devastated. If she's angry, she's furious. She's liable to blow up, slam something, yell and/or cry. Fortunately, she's quick to make up after she cools off. When she's happy, her happiness shines on everyone around her, and when she's unhappy, her black cloud descends just as quickly.

You'll never have to worry about whether she loves you or not. Your feelings woman can't hide her emotions. She looks at you and the love shines in her eyes. She talks to you and the love sounds in her voice. She touches you and the love vibrates in her touch.

She worries about your feelings, about whether you're happy or not. She relates to your emotions in a very real way. If you're sad, she's sad for you. If you're happy, she's happy for you.

The feelings woman craves love and attention and is highly tuned to her own body. She's quick to kiss or hug or express her emotions physically, and shines when it comes to touching or being touched. She's sensitive about how and where and when you touch her. If you want to make points with her, touch a lot.

She prefers comfort to style and doesn't go out of her way to dress up. She's more likely to wear warm-ups or old jeans than a cocktail dress and high heels.

Long meetings and discussions make her impatient. She prefers relaxing, and just being, to doing anything. The feelings woman is more spontaneous than the auditory or visual woman, who likes to think things over or see how they look first. The feelings woman will do something just because it feels good at the moment, without analyzing or worrying too much about whether it's a good idea or not. For her, whatever feels good is a good idea.

Her spontaneity can ruin your plans, though, because her feelings change and she's liable to say something like "I just don't feel like going to a movie tonight. Why don't we just stay in and order pizza?" You might as well go along with the pizza. If you don't, she'll just be uncomfortable all evening.

She will be very upset if she feels you aren't paying enough attention to her feelings. She wants you to be unhappy, as well as sympathetic, if she's unhappy. She wants you to act as if her feelings are important to you. Missing her feelings can be fatal to your relationship with her.

She needs physical closeness to be happy. All the words in the world won't move her if she doesn't have your physical presence. The best way to make a feelings woman feel loved is to be there, actually beside her, body to body, as much as possible. She's quick to become addicted to your physical presence and will never be satisfied without it.

Your feelings woman enjoys sensual experiences. She loves to eat and drink, be massaged, soak in a hot tub, lie in the sun, and be physically pampered.

The feelings woman is usually a good cook, but don't expect her to be the perfect housekeeper or even just ordinarily neat. Her decor is based on comfort, not style. She's relaxed about life, generally amiable and flexible, easy to love; and she loves easily.

The best way to let a feelings woman know you love her is by your touch and your kiss and by your concern for her comfort and her feelings. Telling her you love her all the time is nice, but she needs to be touched in a certain way to feel loved. By observing her reactions, you'll be able to tell how she likes to be touched. The right touch makes her warm all over.

Feelings Eyes

Your feelings woman looks down a lot, not because she's shy but because she's checking to find out how she feels about a subject. You can tell if she's giving serious thought to something because her eyes will look downward.

She can sense when you're paying attention to her even if she's not looking at you. It may seem as if she's not listening to you because she's not looking at you, but that's not true. She's checking out everything with her inner barometer before she lets you know what she thinks.

Most people tend to look down when you ask them how they feel about something, but the feelings woman looks down and to her right whenever you ask any neutral question that forces her to search her mind.

It's very important not to confuse a feelings woman with a visual or auditory woman. One of my clients almost lost the woman he loved because he didn't recognize that she was a feelings woman. Frank and Elaine had been going out for almost a year when he came to see me. "I don't know what I'm doing wrong," he explained, "but she says I don't give her enough. I give her everything.

"I'm always telling her how much I love her and yet she doesn't seem to really believe me. I've given her my all and she says it's just not enough."

When I saw the couple together, the problem with their relationship immediately became obvious. When they came into my office, Elaine greeted me with a warm touch and Frank stayed away. When they sat on my couch, he sat in the corner and she moved over to be next to him. She reached out to touch him and he pulled farther away. When she put her hand on his knee, he kept his hands in his lap.

Elaine was very much a feelings woman. She wanted to touch Frank all the time, but he was very withdrawn physically. Frank was very auditory, always talking about his feelings but never actually demonstrating them. No wonder Elaine was worried.

When we were alone, she told me, "He says he loves me, but he seems like such a cold fish sometimes. I need more affection. The only time he touches me is when we're making love. Other than in bed, he never demonstrates his love, he just tells me it's there and I should believe him if he tells me he loves me. But I don't. I need more. I'm not going to spend the rest of my life with a cold, unaffectionate man, no matter how much he says he loves me."

Frank's verbal reassurances just weren't enough for Elaine. Once Frank learned to touch Elaine in a loving way when he didn't want sex, but just to let her know he cared in the way that was important to her, their relationship turned around. He had to learn to touch her affectionately during the day for no reason, to kiss her when he came in and when he left, and in the morning and at night.

At first, Frank felt self-conscious, because he had been brought up in a very undemonstrative family, but Elaine reacted so positively that he was encouraged. Soon he was touching Elaine a lot more and learning to reach out and touch others as well. Frank was amazed at how he could break down barriers, even at work, by simply touching someone.

You can tell if your woman is a feelings woman by making simple observations. Watch her eyes for downward movements. Listen to the words she uses. Test her responses to pictures, to sounds, to feelings. The feelings woman always responds best to emotions and sensations.

Feelings Tests

QUESTIONS TO FIND OUT IF SHE'S A FEELINGS WOMAN

(Watch her eye movements and listen to her answers. Check for feelings words and downward eye movements.)

What was your childhood like?
What did you like about your first boyfriend?
What's the best part of your job?
What's the worst part of your job?

QUESTIONS TO INVOKE A FEELINGS REACTION

(Since feelings are felt in the present, even if they're remembered from the past, all feelings, whether current or past, are expressed with downward eye movements.)

Have you ever been in love before?
What do you remember about your grandmother?
What do you think about having children?
Were you ever lost when you were little?
What's the most embarrassing dating experience you've
   ever had?

How to Talk to the Feelings Woman

You talk to the feelings woman with your heart. She prefers feelings words to auditory or visual words. Try to touch her while you're talking. Even though you can convey more to her by touching than by talking, there are certain words and expressions that will get her attention.

By using feelings words, you'll get her to relax and trust you more. You'll eliminate stress and arguments because she'll really understand what you're saying.

What the Feelings Woman Is Likely to Say to You

(The feelings words are in italic.)

Keeping in *touch* with *close* friends makes me *feel warm*
   all over.
I *hate* to *hurt* anyone.
That *hurt* my *feelings.*
I don't *feel* like going to a *cold* football game.
I'd *feel* more *comfortable* in a small, *intimate* place.
My ex was *cold* and *unresponsive.*
Don't you *care* about my *feelings?*
That *experience* left a *sour taste* in my mouth.
I don't *like* him because he seems *cold* and *uptight.*
I have a *feeling* you won't *understand*.
When you *touch* me, it *turns me on.*
If you *loved* me, you'd be more *sensitive.*
When you're *happy, so am I.*
If you're *unhappy,* you won't *enjoy* yourself.
I don't want to *force* you to do something you're going to
   hate.

   When you answer your feelings woman, you should use
feelings words, and maybe a touch. Here are some words
that will get your feelings woman's attention.

What You Should Say to the Feelings Woman

(The feelings words are in italic.)

I can *understand* how you *feel.*
I *love* the way your *body feels.*
I want to *touch* you all the time.
Let's stay home and *relax.*
Let's both *lighten up.*

There's no need to be *upset.*
Holding you is *soothing.*
I *feel secure* when we're together.
I *love* the way you can *sense* my *feelings.*
I *feel uncomfortable* in *cold* climates.
I *like* people who are *warm* and *open.*
My ideal woman is *warm* and *exciting.*
It's important to me to stay in *touch* with old friends.
Let's not *push* each other too *hard.*

If you care more about how things look or sound, using feelings words may seem uncomfortable at first. It may seem awkward for you to use unfamiliar expressions, but this feelings mode will sound natural to her. She's the one who'll be listening and hearing the words that make an impact on her. She'll be delighted to have found someone with whom she can really communicate.

Remember that these are clear, valid, common words. You can express your thoughts just as honestly with feelings words with as any other words. And the effort spent learning to communicate feelings won't be wasted even if you decide you don't like the woman. You can use this technique on any other feelings person with whom it is important for you to communicate. Being able to change gears linguistically makes you a more powerful person.

If the woman you want is a feelings woman, simply changing the words you use is the first step toward winning her. Soon it will be natural for you to use feelings expressions with her. The more you think in terms of feelings, the more you will convince the feelings woman that you really understand and appreciate her. Because you are speaking her language, she'll unconsciously want to agree with what you say.

So if you usually say, "I see what you mean" or "I hear you," try saying, "I understand how you feel." It may sound strange to you, but it will sound perfectly natural to her. If you usually say, "That doesn't sound right to me," try saying, "That doesn't strike me as right."

Feelings words are her love language. Using them will help you avoid misunderstandings and make her feel understood. She'll be closer, more intimate, and more in tune with you. You will have a growing power of persuasion over her.

How the Feelings Woman Spends Her Time

Sunbathing
Being playful and childlike
Crying at sad movies
Getting or giving a massage
Working out
Sympathizing with others
Gardening
Sailing
Dancing
Eating and cooking
Indulging in sensual pursuits
Laughing
Thrill-seeking
Talking about her feelings
Enjoying life

What the Feelings Woman Does for a Living

Psychologist
Doctor
Educator
Minister

Nurse
Chef
Masseuse or physical therapist
Acupuncturist
Counselor
Minister
Hairdresser
Potter
Dentist
Public relations person
Bartender
Animal trainer or breeder

How to Make Love to the Feelings Woman

In bed, your feelings woman is a secret treasure, reacting to every touch, perfectly in tune with you, knowing exactly when to give pleasure and when to receive it.

Your feelings woman may love soft, cuddly moments as well as hard-driving sexual peaks. She enjoys gentle or forceful sex. Usually, she can be turned on by just about anything that feels good. She gets as much pleasure out of making you feel good, so she's eager to please. She loves to experiment and enjoys new experiences.

Your feelings woman will become sexually addicted to you faster than other women because each sensation is more meaningful to her. Getting good sex makes her want more and more.

Don't be shy about expressing yourself physically with her. She loves lots of hugs and kisses and tender caresses. She prefers to touch first and talk later. Throw your arms around her. Rub up against her. Tell her often how good she feels to you.

Since the feelings woman is more attuned to all her

senses—taste and smell as well as touch—be sure you appeal to those senses too. Find out what her favorite aftershave is and wear it. Cook for her and feed her with your fingers.

Wear your soft cashmere sweater and she won't be able to keep her hands off you. Your feelings woman can't resist touching anything, especially if it feels good. Be sure to shave closely when she's coming over. Stubble turns her off even more than it does other women. She likes your skin soft and your beard tamed.

She may not notice how well dressed you are or how good your stereo is, but if you have a lumpy mattress or old scratchy sheets, you'll lose points with her. So bring out your satin sheets, incense, perfumes, massage oils, vibrators, velvet, feathers, and furs. Your feelings woman loves them all.

Use feelings words when you're making love. Tell her, "I love touching the smooth skin on the inside of your thigh." Or "I love the feel of your warm lips on mine."

With your feelings woman, you can let yourself get carried away in the bedroom. Pour chocolate on her and then lick it off. Rub her all over with baby oil. Kiss her everywhere. Experiment with new ways to touch each other. Tell her you love her while you're touching her.

Your feelings woman loves everything slow, slow, slow. Slow lovemaking, long slow strokes, and deep slow breaths. Taking your time means a lot to the feelings woman. If she feels that she's being rushed, she'll turn off. No quickies allowed here. Psychologically, she likes everything deep and slow. Although she's quick to give her heart, she'll still require you to take your time with her.

A feelings woman in my counseling group told me that she had fallen madly in love with a man after the first time they made love. She insisted that no man in the world had ever touched her the way he did.

"It was a warm, heavy evening. We had been out three

times, but we both sensed that this was going to be the night. Everything was perfect.

"He said he'd love to demonstrate his gourmet cooking skills for me, and then afterward, if I wanted, he'd give me a full body massage. He'd just finished a course in massage and had already given me several little tastes of what he had learned. Once he gave me a delicious foot massage, another time he gave me a hand massage, and on our last date he massaged my head and face. So I was really primed for the full body treatment.

"When I arrived at his apartment, he had the air-conditioning turned way up and a fire burning in the fireplace—in the middle of a heat wave. 'I thought it would be fun to pretend it's cold outside,' he said, 'just so we remember how good a fire feels.' Since it was really cold, he loaned me a cashmere sweater and we huddled together drinking wine in front of the fireplace. He was burning my favorite wild gardenia incense and he was wearing my favorite men's cologne, Vetiver by Guerlain.

"I was bowled over by all the sensations. Then he served the most delicious meal. Stuffed mushrooms for an hors d'oeuvre, lobster for the main course, and chocolate mousse for dessert. I was totally swept away before we even got to the massage.

"Between each course, he kissed me in the most amazingly tender way, touching my face and lips with his fingers as if he was admiring, almost worshipping me. I felt like a fairy princess being adored by her long-lost prince.

"Then after kissing me all over, he brought out his massage table, put on some strange meditation music, and lit cinnamon-scented candles all over the room. Starting with my toes, he massaged every inch of my body, front and back, with warmed massage oil. I have never felt such a rush of sensation.

"Afterward, we began to explore each other's bodies, to feel the different parts together. His face brushed on my thigh, and I felt his gentle lips, his soft beard, even his eyelashes. My cheek brushed the hair on his chest, my tongue felt rough on his softness.

"Then, slowly, we were drawn into each other's bodies, tongue to tongue, lips to lips, and we became one.

"I haven't been able to think about anything else since, except getting close to him again, feeling his body against mine, his sweet touch and gentle lips. I get all tingly just thinking about him."

Remember, when you want to turn your feelings woman on, touch first and talk later. If you want her to listen, she'll listen better when you're making her feel good. If you want her to notice something, show it to her when you're touching her. Start by getting on her wavelength, then add your own.

What You Are

Visual Man. If you are very neat, if the things in your closet and on your dresser are lined up in rows, if you are more of a Type A personality—high-strung, workaholic, foot-jiggling, always moving around—you are probably a visual man. You prefer looking at a map to hearing directions told to you. You prefer to see something first, and will decide if you like it based on whether it looks good to you or not.

Visual Man/Feelings Woman. If you're a visual man, you could become frustrated by the feelings woman's lack of order and neatness. On the other hand, you could live a lot longer with a feelings woman by getting in tune with her relaxed state. Instead of being frustrated by her lack of visual perception, you can benefit from her intuitive good sense. She'll never run off to chase a pretty face either, because once the feelings woman loves, she loves your soul.

Auditory Man. You could well be an engineer and high-tech type. That's because your mind is so organized. You are a logical thinker. Not exactly a fashion plate, you prefer casual clothes to dressy ones. You are not known for neatness and your sense of style. You are a good talker and listener and decide things based on how they sound.

Auditory Man/Feelings Woman. If you're an auditory man, you'll enjoy spending time with the feelings woman because she's such a sympathetic and responsive listener. You can reach her by talking about your feelings. Try communicating with her nonverbally too, and always touch her when you're talking to make sure she's listening.

Feelings Man. You are the most sensitive and the most in touch with your feelings of all men. You are mellower, slower-moving, and would rather be comfortable than anything else. You like to touch a lot, and make your decisions based on how things feel. Your emotions are close to the surface. You love eating and sleeping and soft furs and your favorite chair.

Feelings Man/Feelings Woman. If you're a feelings man, you're in luck if you find a woman who is a feelings woman. The two of you will sense each other's needs and communicate easily with a touch. You won't need words or pictures to get close. The feelings woman is as sensitive as you are. She'll share your joys and pain, hurting when you hurt and being happy when you're happy.

Mirroring

Trust is one of the most important ingredients in love. Mirroring is a simple but powerful technique you can use with any woman to get her to start trusting you.

Trust

People tend to trust other people who are like them and to mistrust people who seem different. That, unfortunately, is one reason why there's so much prejudice in the world. We are often suspicious of people just because they have different skin color or different accents. Imagine how hard it is for a woman to trust a man—the opposite sex. Men are intimidating to women, a mystery. Lots of women are afraid of men because they've had bad experiences in the past. There are techniques you can use to overcome many of a woman's fears. Mirroring is one of the most powerful. It works on her subconscious, and she'll never know you've done anything.

Similarity and Closeness

Have you ever noticed how lovers tend to look alike?
Couples who are really clicking together resemble each
other in a startling way. It's not just that they start to wear
clothes of the same style and color. They sit alike. They
talk alike. They have similar gestures and body language.
Even their nervous habits, like foot-jiggling or cuticle-
picking, are the same. They definitely march to the beat
of the same drummer.

When I give lectures or appear on TV talk shows, everyone is always amazed when I point out the long-time
couples in the audience. Unaware of it, they are sitting in
the same physical position. The expressions on their faces
are the same. And, of course, their clothes have a similar
style and color.

It's not just because she buys his clothes or wears his
favorite color. It's because they are truly in tune. People
in love act alike without even thinking about it consciously. People in love always admire the other person.
They want to please the other person and so they unconsciously emulate him or her. Often, just by watching a
couple together, you can tell the exact state of their relationship. Do they sit in the same position? Do they look
alike? Do they sound alike?

You can even tell, before they know themselves, when
couples are about to break up. Couples who aren't really
together tend to put physical distance between themselves. They sit differently and dress differently and
hardly ever touch.

Even when you're not in love, you'll notice that your
friends are a lot like you. They have the same intellectual
capacity, education, and interests, and they often work in
the same field. You feel most comfortable with others like
yourself. We all do. We tend to seek out others whose
tastes and values are like ours.

Men and women both like and trust the familiar. The

most familiar is themselves, which is why people are attracted to other people just like themselves.

When you find a woman whose love you want, look for and emphasize the similarities between the two of you. Dwell on how alike you are, on your similar interests—you both like to wear jeans, say, or you both love old movies. De-emphasize the differences. Then she'll automatically trust you and begin to feel close to you.

Lots of men object to this, saying, "Wait a minute. That's dishonest. Besides, I don't want to have to conform myself to her for her to fall in love with me; I want her to love the real me."

First of all, mirroring is not being dishonest; it's being adaptable. Second, by being adaptable in this way, you are not so much conforming to another person as gaining power over them. (This technique works great in business too, by the way.) Third, in order for her to experience the "real" you, you'll first have to get close to her and communicate with her in a way she can understand.

Physical Mirroring

Mirroring a woman's physical appearance is one of the most powerful techniques for getting close, and you can learn it instantly with no training. If you use nothing else in this whole book, physical mirroring alone will make a huge difference in the way women react when you approach them. If you are the least bit skeptical about the techniques in this book, try this one first. You'll be amazed at the results. All you have to do is sit or stand in the same position as the woman you want to get close to.

The next time you're at a party and you see a woman you want to meet, try mirroring. Begin by really getting in sync with her. Stop thinking about yourself and your bald spot; stop worrying whether she seems to like you or not, whether you're doing the right things or not. Begin thinking about her, and watching her, and getting in sync with her. Because women are traditionally trying so hard to get in sync with a man, she'll never guess that it's you who are doing the connecting.

Say she's sitting in a chair holding a drink in one hand. If she's sitting back in her chair, you sit back in yours and hold your drink more or less the same way. If she's leaning forward, you lean forward. Even if she crosses her arms in front of her in the "don't get near me" body posture, don't be daunted. Cross your arms in front of you too. But be subtle about it; this is not a game of monkey see, monkey do. Say she crosses one leg over the other one and starts to tap her foot in time with the music. Casually, as if it has just occurred to you, cross your legs a few seconds after she crosses hers and tap your finger in time with the music.

If she notices anyone in the room, it will be you. She won't know why, but she'll feel drawn to you, as if she wanted to get to know you, as if she were unconsciously sure that the two of you would hit it off. The reason is that her unconscious senses the harmony you've created between the two of you.

You don't have to be the most outgoing guy in town. You don't have to be the life of the party, full of jokes and cute lines. And you certainly don't have to be rich and handsome to make mirroring work for you.

By using the technique of mirroring properly, you won't have to worry whether a woman is receptive to you. She'll be ready to talk to you before you even say hello. She'll be primed to like you, ready to trust you, and eager to get to know you better. Mirroring is so effective that women often make passes at the men who are mirroring them.

The man who is mirroring a woman stands out because he is so different from the other men in the room. Most men are into themselves—how they're standing, sitting, talking; their opening line, what they're going to say next; and, finally, what the woman thinks of them. Actually, most women think most men are cute but inflexible, stubborn and stuck in their own perceptions of how things should be. In order to break out of that mold, use mirroring.

Remember, for it to work best, mirroring shouldn't be mechanical or quick. It should be subtle, smooth, and unnoticed. Allow a second or two to pass before you change your position to hers. Then drift into a matching posture as though you were unconsciously drawn into it. Naturally, you shouldn't mirror a disability like a twitch or limp, but any normal body posture is okay to mirror.

Mirroring will work on anyone with whom you want to have better rapport, so practice on your friends and family until you are able to mirror someone's body movements easily and smoothly. Some of your friends will feel closer to you immediately. Others will mirror you back. Some, you may notice, are already mirroring you. You hardly get a chance to mirror them. These are the people who automatically mirror anyone. They are often people you can confide in and trust.

Some natural "mirrorers" are extremely successful in sales. Remember the last time you overbought stereo equipment or spent too much on clothes? I'll bet the salesman seemed to understand your needs and was someone you felt you really liked. He or she was probably mirroring you, your voice, your movements, your unconscious body rhythms. That made you feel trusting and probably encouraged you to spend more easily than you would have otherwise.

Studies have shown that you can tell a lot more by studying a man or woman's body language than by listening to the words he or she says. When you first meet, a woman has an agenda of things she wants you to know about her and things she doesn't want you to know. By studying her body language, you can tell whether she likes you, whether she's ready to agree to anything, or whether she wants you to get lost. You can even tell if she's lying.

Most guys know the classic and most obvious example of this. She's next to you, lying back on the couch. Her eyes are dilated and she's breathing heavily. "We'd better stop," she says. And, of course, her body language is telling you not to stop.

Another familiar example. You've just had a very nice first date with a woman you hope to see again. She says she had a really good time and she'll be seeing you soon. But her arms are crossed in front of her and she isn't making much eye contact with you. You know you can forget about seeing her again.

A woman has a lot more control over what she says than over her body language. When her body language and what she says contradict each other, you should always believe the body language. It's the key to how she really feels.

Extend your mirroring as you get to know a woman. Don't feel limited to body posture. Mirror habits, even speech. You may wonder if she won't suspect what you're doing. Not if you are subtle. If she's soft-spoken and you're not, she may notice that you're speaking more softly when you're with her, but she'll assume you are strongly affected by her and under the spell of her good influence. What could be more endearing?

She'll be thrilled and excited by the unconscious harmony you've created just by subtly matching her. In a subtle way, you'll be showing that you agree with her. For the same reason, if you act and look the exact opposite of her, then unconsciously she'll get the message that you disagree with how she looks and acts. Your being like her validates her values and ideals, assuming she likes herself.

If she doesn't like herself, you'll have a hard time convincing her that you like her, no matter what you do. It's best to start out with someone who has good self-esteem. That way she's going to like you if you're like her.

The next step is to check your rapport with the woman you've been mirroring. See if you can lead her. When you're in sync with her, after you've followed her with physical mirroring for a few minutes, change your position and see if she changes hers to follow you. If she does, that means you're doing a good job of getting close, that she's receptive to you, and that this is a good time to ask for what you want. On the other hand, if she doesn't follow you, then go back to following her. After you're sure you're both in sync, try again to get her to follow you.

By studying her movements, you will learn her own special rhythm, how she breathes, when she's ready to follow you anywhere. You will have the key to creating conscious harmony with her whenever your relationship strays off-center, enabling you to bring both of you back to a loving, in-sync, together place whenever you want.

What Shall I Wear?

Physical mirroring has a lot to do with the way you dress as well as with the way you act. You should dress compatibly with the woman you want to win. No, this doesn't mean you wear panty hose. It means you dress so that you two will look as if you came to the party together. In other words, if she's into denim, wear denim. If she's into Calvins, wear Calvins. Within reason, dress like her.

Example: You've made a date with her for a party. You already know she loves dressy silks and fancy fabrics and sparkling looks. Call her a couple of days ahead and ask her, "Shall we dress to kill?" Then don't let her down. Wear your best suit, silk tie, and dress shoes. If you know she prefers warm-ups to anything else, ask her, "How much can we underdress for this thing and still get in the door?" She'll love you for it.

The simple act of collaborating on what you're going to wear accomplishes many objectives, all at once. First of all, she'll appreciate it. Women are resigned to guys being generally oblivious to the whole subject of clothes. So if you call to coordinate, she'll think you're thoughtful and sensitive. She can quit worrying about what the hell you're going to show up in and start looking forward to the date. Second, it's fun to be in collusion. When you arrive at a party in compatible outfits you've planned out ahead of time, the date takes on a subtle added dimension. There's just the beginning of that "us against the world" feeling.

The same principle holds even on the first or second date, before you know her quite well enough to collaborate. If she leans toward punk, be a little punk; it won't kill you. It's hard enough to get close and feel at ease with a new woman without wearing something that fights her image and tells her you don't like the way she dresses.

What if you've seen her only at the office and you don't know how she dresses elsewhere? Simple. If your first date is for a movie, then just wear something fairly normal and appropriate for a movie date. This is not the best time to surprise her with the "other" you, who dresses like Elton John every time you get away from the office.

All of the above is true even if you haven't yet met the woman of your dreams and you just want to be prepared. Check your Woman Plan. If you want a high-powered, always-together type, make it a point to do shopping and errand-running on your way home from the office, and keep your jacket and tie on. When your shopping cart bumps into Ms. Right's, she'll be more likely to start a conversation than if you're dressed like Joe Schlump. She will be attracted to you because you're like her.

Once, when my husband and I were dating, he invited me to a party that included other women he was seeing.

I didn't have the vaguest idea what to wear—my sexiest, my boldest, my finest, or most casual, as if I really didn't care that much. So I called him and asked him what he was going to wear. He said, "I don't know, probably just a silk shirt and jeans." That's exactly what I wore.

All night long he couldn't stop looking at me. He forgot that I'd asked him what he was going to wear and never imagined that I'd worn the same thing intentionally. He just thought I was oh so chic, dressed exactly right for the occasion. One of my rivals wore a slinky Halston, and the other a sexy bare-midriff gypsy outfit, but he was hardly impressed. What he liked best was my matching him. He never knew until much much later that I was mirroring him that night.

Once you stop thinking about yourself and start thinking about the woman you want to win, you'll discover many ways to mirror her. For example, you can make her feel more comfortable at your place if you buy her brands of soap and toothpaste.

Now, many men wouldn't consider doing that. They are adamant about not changing a thing for a woman. "Either she takes me the way I am, or too bad." Often, it's "too bad, Charlie."

This is something to keep in perspective. Is your particular style of dress more important than being compatible with a woman you definitely want? Probably not. We're not talking about changing your basic values here. We're talking about what you wear on certain occasions, and about soap and toothpaste. Mirroring doesn't mean you change the person you are. The real you will shine through no matter what.

After all, most men adapt to their surroundings to some degree, even if they're not aware of it. If you're an executive, you probably wear a business suit every day to go to work, and maybe you wear warm-ups after work. But if you go to a country-western bar, you'll naturally think about wearing something different, maybe jeans and a plaid shirt. To some extent, mirroring is something we all do unconsciously to fit in. Understanding it and making it work with the woman of your choice are important. If you want her to choose you, she has to see you fitting into her lifestyle.

If you feel very strongly about your particular style—how you dress, what you wear, even the brand of toothpaste you use—then don't change. If you feel undressed in anything but a three-piece suit, and yet you're hot for a woman whose favorite outfit is jeans and an old shirt, maybe you're hot for the wrong woman. Reevaluate your Woman Plan. Look for a woman who's more like you. Just keep in mind that bringing a woman into your life is going to require some flexibility and adaptability. Men who find it impossible to compromise on any issue, not just what they wear, are the ones who wind up single and lonely.

On the other hand, if you can be flexible, if you're willing to try new things, you will find that mirroring gives you power. You will gain new insight into other people. You will be able to communicate more effectively and to influence people in all areas of your life. And nowhere does mirroring work better than in a new relationship with a woman.

Mirroring is a way to emphasize the similarities between you and the woman you want. She'll begin to identify with you, to feel that you and she are members of a very special and elite club, that you are soul mates on a deeper level. Then she is more likely to agree with your suggestions, she is easier to convince, and she is more likely to return your love.

Mirroring should not threaten your sense of self. Changing what you wear, the way you sit or communicate, does not mean changing who you are. It simply makes you more powerful, especially with women. Try it. It's easy. It's fun. It works.

Advanced Mirroring

There's more to a woman than how she looks or how she sounds. There's a rhythm, a beat—a quick, perky one or a slow, sensual one. Sometimes the rhythm changes, but there's a particular one she finds normal and comfortable most of the time. That's the speed at which she tends to lead her life. It may be frenetic or lazy, but it's there, and chances are it's there for good.

Mirroring Rhythms

In order to make a baby feel comfortable, a new invention mimics the beat of the mother's heart. New kittens are made to feel at home by the ticking of a clock in their beds. All animals are in tune with an unconscious rhythm. Find a woman's rhythm and you'll have a way to reach her on a very subtle, subconscious level.

137

The visual woman tends to move fast and talk fast. The auditory woman will move a bit slower. And the feelings woman is the most mellow, least hyper of the three. If you're a feelings man interested in a visual, fast-talking woman, you don't need to speed up the pace of your whole life, but you can try talking a bit faster when you're with her. If you do, she'll feel more more comfortable and happier when you're around, without really knowing why.

If she's a feelings woman, more slow-talking, just slow down a little when you're with her. That's the simplest form of mirroring a woman's rhythm.

By mirroring the speed of your woman's speech and the rhythm of her movements, you'll get in tune with her. This kind of mirroring is more subtle than physical mirroring. It's not necessarily the movement, but the pace of the movement that is mirrored.

Observe her less obvious, more unconscious rhythms. Does she jiggle her foot? Is she a finger-tapper? Then, unobtrusively and subtly, adapt one of her rhythms into one of your own. You don't have to duplicate her physical movement exactly. Create a movement of your own that is similar in pace. For example, if she's tapping her fingers, bounce your foot in the same rhythm. She'll never notice.

While you are mirroring her rhythm, begin to observe her breathing.

Mirroring Breathing

Have you ever noticed how, in the afterglow of making love, when you're lying in each other's arms—half conscious, half drifting, still hot but with your passions spent—there is a wonderful feeling of union, of belonging together? You feel remarkably close, perhaps even closer than when you were making love. The intimacy of that

moment is intensified by the natural, unconscious tend- ✓
ency to breathe together in unison.

Some Eastern philosophies believe that breath is the
life force and that by breathing like another person you
become a part of that person's life. Tantric yogis practice
breathing in and out together in perfect unison during sex
to enhance their feelings of oneness.

Breathing in unison happens more often than we realize during intense shared activities. Watch men lifting
weights. One will lift, and the other will help with the
weights and urge the lifter to lift more. Notice how the
man who is helping the lifter adopts the lifter's breathing
pattern.

By learning to mirror breathing, you can create a subtle
feeling of intimacy between you and another person, anytime, anywhere.

You can use the secret of breathing in unison to create
a feeling of closeness on demand. You don't have to wait
until you've finished making love to be close. Actually, it's
better if you and she start getting close before you get into
bed. In fact, you can start at the first meeting by breathing
like she does.

To find the rhythm of her breathing, watch her shoulders. If you can't see any movement, try focusing on a
spot behind her shoulders. Watch the slight change as
they move with her breathing. Notice the difference
between her breathing and yours. Does she breathe
faster or slower than you? Is she a shallow breather or a
deep breather? If you want to get really close really
fast, breathing together is the best way. A woman feels   ✓
safe and trusting with a man who breathes the way she
does.

You can also use breathing in her rhythm as a way of
restoring harmony when you've had a disagreement. Like
physical mirroring, the mirroring of rhythms and breathing creates an unconscious harmony that the other person
wants to continue.

Mirroring Life Rhythms

It's really wonderful, and you're very lucky, if the woman you fall in love with has the same life rhythms that you do. Unfortunately, this doesn't always happen. You like to stay up late. She likes to go to bed early. You like to sleep in. She wakes up with the birdies.

Even the best, most in-love couples have problems with different life rhythms. One's a couch potato and the other insists on running five miles a day. One's a party person and the other hates gatherings of more than two good friends.

Once people have fallen in love, they are able to work out these problems, or learn to live with them, because they love each other so much. But in the beginning of a relationship, before they have really fallen for each other, a difference in life rhythms can seem like an insurmountable obstacle.

Recently a couple came to me with a problem of different life rhythms. Even though they claimed they really loved each other, they were both very angry. Judy claimed that she was constantly being pushed into Sam's routine. "I want to relax in the morning. I like to get a slow start on the day. Otherwise I get nervous. But Sam won't let me. He jumps out of bed and starts doing push-ups. Then he wants to go jogging. In the beginning of our relationship, he would just go off and do his thing and leave me in bed asleep. But lately, he wakes me and wants me to go with him."

"It's for her own good," Sam insisted. "Besides, I want us to spend time together. I'm just trying to share the best part of the day with her."

"That's the best part of the day for him," Judy countered, "but not for me. I'd like us to have a little fun at night, but he gets up so early that he's ready to go to bed at ten o'clock. Whenever we're invited to a party, we're always the first to come and the first to leave because Sam has to get up early and work out."

You might think that Sam and Judy just weren't compatible, but they both swore that they were in love and deeply committed, that there was nobody else they wanted, and that they wanted to stay together.

Sam, who was older than Judy and more worried about his health and stress, soon came to understand that he was causing more stress by badgering Judy about joint morning exercise than he would have by changing his routine. Rather than exercise in the morning, Sam agreed to exercise in the early evening. Judy agreed to exercise with him, so long as it was late in the day.

Now they have comfortable, relaxed mornings and some evenings out. By learning to get in sync with each other's life rhythms, Sam and Judy brought harmony to their relationship. Soon after, they were married.

To get a woman to change and do something you want, to modify her rhythm to match yours, you must first get into a state of agreement with her by matching your rhythm to hers. Think of a sports car racer downshifting to slow his car. First, the engine must be revved up to match the speed of the car; then, once the gears are meshed, the engine can slow the car.

Once you've matched her rhythm, the two of you are in sync. You are in a state of agreement that is pleasant for her. Then, as you gradually change your rhythm, she will be drawn along, unconsciously trying to maintain that pleasant state of agreement. She will not feel at all forced.

Getting in tune with your woman's life rhythms is very important, especially in the beginning, when a woman is looking at you and wondering if she could possibly spend the rest of her life with you. She wants to know that you are flexible, that you are willing to make changes for her, and that there is a strong feeling of harmony between the two of you.

So, if the woman you want is a quiet, stay-at-home type, don't try to drag her out to the disco right away. Have some quiet times with her first, and then ease her into the disco scene. If she's a party animal, try being a party animal first, and then show her some quiet times.

Naturally, if all this is too much for you, if you just can't be quiet with a quiet woman or be a party animal with Miss "girls just wanna have fun," then you may want to review your Woman Plan and rethink how it happened that you're seriously dating someone so totally incompatible.

Remember, if you steadfastly refuse to compromise, and insist on always doing everything your way, she may change her life for you—temporarily. Eventually, though, she'll resent always having to give in, and she'll come to resent you too. Also, you will be denying yourself the pleasure of gaining another perspective on life.

Mirroring Volume

If you've fallen for a woman who's a quiet type, who never talks above a whisper or raises her voice in anger, you should be quiet too. She'll be most responsive to you if you match your volume and intensity to hers. A loud or very intense approach could embarrass or annoy her and make her want to pull away from you.

So if you're a man with a big, booming voice, try lowering the volume when you're with a woman who talks softly. A man who talks much louder than a woman can come off looking like a volume bully—someone who always gets his way by outshouting whomever he's with.

If you're a quiet, soft-spoken man with a mellow, modulated voice and you're attracted to a rowdy, life-of-the-party woman with a loud voice, try speaking louder when you approach her. Remember that if you're too quiet, you can be as off-putting for a loud, emotional woman as a loudmouth is for a quiet woman.

Warren and Jill came to me for help with their relationship. They really cared for each other, but they were having a lot of trouble communicating. As soon as I met them, I could see what the problem was. Jill was loud. Her voice was high-pitched and emotional. You could easily hear how upset she was.

Warren, on the other hand, was just as upset. Only his being upset didn't show at all in his voice. He refused to fight with Jill or even discuss things much of the time because she got emotional and screamed. He never raised his voice. He talked slowly and quietly.

Jill had done just about everything she could think of to get Warren to argue or get mad—to react in an emotional way—so that she would be convinced he cared. "He's so uncommunicative and unemotional about things, I feel like he doesn't care about me at all," she told me. "He won't even say 'I love you.'"

Warren calmly informed her, "I'm here, aren't I. You can tell how I feel or I wouldn't be here in therapy trying to work things out with you."

But Jill didn't feel loved because Warren's feelings didn't show in his voice. Her attempts to draw him out by picking fights, and screaming and yelling, only made him withdraw more. Warren and Jill were caught in a vicious circle in which Jill became more insecure and demanding and Warren became more withdrawn. Their entire relationship was threatened.

When Jill was able to calm down vocally, and when Warren learned to say "I love you" (the words she so desperately needed to hear) and to speak a little louder, their problems were easier to work out. As long as each spoke in a different volume, the other one felt threatened. As soon as Warren learned to yell back once in a while, Jill felt as if he really cared. Jill soon decided, though, that she didn't care for screaming and yelling when they were directed at her, and she began to quiet down.

You can change a woman's behavior the way Warren changed Jill's, but you must first be willing to change your own behavior and get in tune with her. Then, once she feels comfortable with you and trusts you because you're so much like her, she'll be willing to let you lead and to let her behavior follow yours.

Mirroring Belief Systems

Agreement is the key to getting close. Whenever you want to convince a woman to do something or to believe something, begin with an area of agreement. Get on the same side first. She'll like the harmony and togetherness you have created. She'll want to maintain that harmonious feeling, and so she'll be more likely to want to agree with you.

Remember, conflict breeds more conflict, and agreement breeds agreement. Set a tone of fighting in your relationship and you'll be plagued with fights until you break up. Set a tone of agreement in your relationship and you'll be able to work out the differences when they come along.

This doesn't mean that you should lie or say a lot of things you don't mean. Lies can come back to haunt you and will decay the trust in a relationship. Being in agreement means emphasizing the areas in which you agree and de-emphasizing the areas in which you disagree.

Surely there must be something you agree on. Otherwise, why are you together? Thinking about the areas of agreement will keep you positive about your relationship. Dwelling on the areas of disagreement tends to make you feel negative about it. The same goes for her too. So if you want a woman to feel good about your relationship, present as many areas of agreement as you can.

Always telling the truth can be difficult too. Sometimes you know that she doesn't really want to hear the truth, or that she'll get very angry if you do tell her something. "All's fair in love and war" may be true. The problem is that when she finds out what you've done that's unfair, she'll be furious.

Let's say, for instance, that you're going out with a woman who loves ethnic music, food, and clothes. Nothing makes her happier than to get all dressed up in a sari and go to an Indian restaurant or to go to an Arab café and clap for the belly dancers.

In the beginning of the relationship you pretend to enjoy the whole ethnic routine just a little more than you really do, because you want to be agreeable and because it makes her so happy and responsive to you. Now you find yourself on a steady diet of ethnic cuisine and drums of one sort or another every weekend. She's even planning your next vacation at the Belly Dancers of America convention in Las Vegas.

How do you break it to her that your stomach's on fire and your brains are vibrating and your ears can't stand another evening of tambourines? You don't want her to feel as if you've hated all those evenings you've spent clapping, singing, and dancing; but you've had it. You're dying for a steak house with new-wave music.

Don't suddenly blurt out, "I hate belly dancing, I hate spicy food, and I've never liked drums. The very thought of another night in a smoke-filled room of whirling dervishes makes me sick. Can't we ever do anything I want to do?"

Instead, control your urge to put an end to the shish kebab pilaf once and for all. Whether it's sex or Chinese food, expressing dissatisfaction with what you've been doing for some time is sure to bring trouble. She's going to think you've been pretending to like belly dancing and God knows what else. How can she ever believe you again?

Begin by getting into an area of agreement. Start by saying something like "I really enjoy our evenings of music, belly dancers, and spicy food." Now you have your woman agreeing with you. Then you say, "But lately, I've been having an overwhelming desire for prime rib."

Because you've started out mirroring her belief system about ethnic foods, she is receptive to your idea. Without lying or compromising yourself, you have begun the discussion in an agreeable way. Then, after getting her into a pattern of agreement, you can bring up the disagreement.

Let's suppose you want a woman you're dating to do something special in bed, something she has never shown any particular interest in—say, anal or oral stimulation. First, never complain about the sex you are getting. Always say it's wonderful. Let her know how much you're enjoying the lovemaking the two of you share; let her know how much she excites you and how desirable you think she is. That way, you are starting from a point of agreement—that you both like the sex you have. After that, it's much easier to get her to do something different.

Mirroring belief systems and getting into agreement with a woman are no big deal. You go to your doctor and the first thing he does is get into agreement with you. "Let's see," he says. "You've got a pain in your elbow." You nod yes. "And you've had it for two months?" Again you agree. "Well," he says, "I'm going to fix you right up." Which isn't necessarily true, but you tend to agree with him because he's gotten you into a state of agreement first.

Getting into agreement with a woman can be anything from "You need to relax this weekend" to "You deserve a shopping spree" to "You need a romantic getaway." You can agree with a woman about anything; the important thing is to emphasize the areas of agreement. Then she will begin to trust you the way a patient trusts a doctor.

There are unlimited possibilities for mirroring. Mirror the rhythm of your lover's sentences, the blinking of her eyes, the way she licks her lips, her breathing, her values, her belief systems, and the way she communicates—and you'll soon be leading her toward you. She'll follow you anywhere.

Anchoring Your Love

I t's amazing. One minute she's adorable, sweet, and loving, your little angel, the girl of your dreams. And then suddenly she turns into the monster from outer space. If only you could push a button and turn Ms. Grump back into Ms. Lovely. Well, you can. With a technique called "anchoring."

Let's face it, no relationship is without its ups and downs. Anchoring is a way to make warm, loving feelings available on call, to bring back the good feelings whenever they start to slip away, to keep the romance alive, and to remind her of how much she cares for you and how wonderful you are whenever she seems about to forget.

Anchoring Happy Feelings

Give your loved one a special touch—a little stroke on her face, a touch on her hair, a special squeeze of her hand—

148

and you can anchor a good feeling she's having. That means you'll be able to reactivate that special feeling any time by using the same touch again.

Here's how it works. Each time she's feeling really good—she's just had a great orgasm or maybe eaten a delicious and romantic dinner—you touch a particular spot on her body in a special way. A warm pressure, a gentle stroke, a loving pat—whatever is comfortable for you. Use this special touch consistently and you are anchoring her good feelings.

Each time the two of you are especially close and she is really happy with you, you can preserve the moment by anchoring it. Sometimes an anchor works immediately, but it's best to repeat the anchor several times. Then when she's less than delighted with you or with life in general, you can easily bring back her good feelings and make her happy again. All you do is touch the same spot in the same way and she'll unconsciously recall being happy and feeling good. You'll be able to evoke the good times and erase the bad ones with your anchor. It's very Pavlovian, but it really works.

Just as certain gestures and touches have come to have special meaning (a touch on the upper arm for comfort in bereavement, a hug for a warm greeting, a pat on the rear for touchdown congratulations), your touch will have special meaning for you and the woman you love. Pick a spot other than the upper arm, since that's already taken. Pick a spot you can reach easily and without embarrassment in any situation. You never know when she'll have an attack of the nasties and need you for an "anchoring attitude adjustment."

Anchoring with a touch should be combined with a vocal anchor as well. Say her name or a pet name in a special tone of voice at the same time you touch the special spot. Be sure you have a pleasant expression on your face, just in case she's looking. Soon all you'll have to do to improve her mood and make her feel more loving is to look pleasant, say her name in a certain tone of voice, and touch the secret spot.

Once you've set the anchor, you can use it anytime to bring back those loving feelings when they start to slip. Let's say you show up to take her out and you can tell she's in a rotten mood. Nothing you did, but you know it will ruin your evening if she doesn't stop acting so miserable.

The worst thing you can do is to tell her everything's fine. It isn't and she knows it. Besides, when she's feeling bad, you should mirror her bad mood and get in tune with it first.

You could say to the visual woman, "I can see why you're upset." Or, to the auditory woman, "I can hear how upset you are." Or, to the feelings woman, "I can understand how you feel." Then, when you've gotten in tune with her miserable mood, the anchor will help you turn her misery to happiness.

At that point you could say, "Oh, honey, that's terrible, I feel so bad for you. It's a shame you don't feel better . . ." (now touch the anchor) ". . . because it's going to be a wonderful evening, and we'll go out, have a nice dinner, and forget about business for a while."

If you've ever felt out of control in a relationship, anchoring can make you feel more in control, even sexually.

Anchoring Sexy Feelings

It's possible to have different anchors for different feelings. For example, you have an anchor you use when you want to make her feel happy. You can have a different anchor to make her feel sexy.

The sex anchor is one of the most powerful anchors you can use. Once it is set up, you'll be amazed at how well it works. Anchoring sexy feelings is very much like an-

choring happy ones, except that the sex anchor is most
effective when you tie it to the moment of her orgasm.

For instance, you're in bed with the woman you love
and she's exploding with passion. She's moaning in ec-
stasy, absolutely palpitating with pleasure. Just at that
moment you kiss her neck. At the same time you say
something that is special to her—her name or a pet name,
and how sexy and wonderful she is. "Sugar, sugar, you're
the greatest." Or "Oh, baby, nobody turns me on like you
do." You, of course, will have to figure out your own special words. (Or you might want to just growl, which one
man reported worked fine.) Then, when you're out to
dinner and you want to make sure you're going to have
a hot and exciting evening when you get home, you can
lean over, kiss her neck, and say the words "Sugar, sugar,
you're the greatest."

Anchoring also works if you do it right after her orgasm.
You could add your own little personal and private twist.
Perhaps you always lick her nipples right after her orgasm, or you might run your fingers up and down her
back, or you could stay inside her while doing all of the
above. Almost all women complain that there's no afterplay. Men withdraw quickly. Women take more time to
get back to normal after orgasm. Anchoring can be con-
sidered afterplay insurance. It insures that you'll get a
chance to play again.

Anchoring to Solve Problems

PROBLEM: SHE TURNS GRUMPY HALFWAY THROUGH
THE EVENING FOR SOME UNKNOWN REASON.

If you've ever had a date turn sour halfway through the
evening, you can use anchoring to get it back on track
again. Even if you haven't had a chance to use a happy

anchor or a sexy anchor with her, you can ask her questions about when she's been really happy. For instance, "What was the best vacation you ever had?" Or "What was the neatest romantic time you ever had?" Or "What do you really enjoy doing?" Or "What turns you on?" Simple questions for a guy to ask. And when she's answering, guess what? She's thinking about all the things that have made her happy, and she's looking at you. Subconsciously, therefore, she's identifying you with all those happy things.

PROBLEM: SHE GETS NEGATIVE ABOUT YOUR RELATIONSHIP JUST WHEN YOU ARE FEELING GOOD—ALL BECAUSE OF SOME ROTTEN GUY IN HER PAST.

Perhaps you're enjoying a terrific relationship with a wonderful woman and you'd like to talk to her about being more committed. You notice that every time you bring up the subject, she pulls back and acts strangely. After a while, you drag out of her that she's been hurt so many times in prior relationships that she can't possibly stand the pain of getting close and getting hurt again.

Most of the time she's terrific, and you're crazy about her. Whenever you try to get closer, though, she remembers the old pain and pulls away, which keeps you insecure and off balance, worried about her possibly leaving you. It really bugs you that some louse from her past is butting into your relationship, even on a thought level. It's as if the jerk were deliberately keeping you and your woman apart. You'd like to punch him out, but of course he's not there. Use anchoring to punch his evil actions out of her mind.

I taught one man to use the technique of "negative anchoring" to get the woman he loved to marry him.

Stephanie and Alex had dated for two years and then had lived together for three. They had a two-year-old daughter, but Stephanie steadfastly refused to marry Alex because her previous marriages had worked out so badly. Whenever he asked her, she'd say, "I love you, and I'm perfectly happy the way things are. Please, let's not change anything." He knew she was thinking of the way the other men had treated her. No matter how much Alex insisted that he wouldn't abandon her or abuse her the way the prior husbands had, Stephanie wouldn't agree to marry him.

Of course, he had been doing exactly the wrong thing. While she was looking at him, he talked about how badly those other men had treated her, making her anchor those bad experiences to him. I taught him to anchor the other men's bad behavior away from himself. It went something like this.

While he was rubbing the back of her neck (the happy feelings anchor he had already set up with her), Alex told Stephanie, "You know, honey, I can picture us growing old together. I feel like we're going to be together forever. I know it would be right for us to get married." Then he felt her stiffen and get ready to tell him the usual about how bad marriage was for love.

He let her finish and he didn't argue with her at all. In fact, he agreed (mirroring her belief system). "You're absolutely right about those men," he told her. "Some men are really bad for women and should never be married." At that point, Alex walked over to a seldom-used chair in the corner of the room and put his hand on the chair. "Those are the men who hurt women."

Then he stepped away from the chair (where he had anchored her bad feelings) and said, "Then there are men like me, nice men, kind men." And as he said this he put the same hand he had put on the chair on his own chest, indicating he was one of the nice guys. "Some men really mean what they say when they say 'I love you'; men like that are loyal to a woman and really do believe in staying together forever."

By anchoring Stephanie's bad feelings to the chair and then physically moving away from the chair and using the same hand to indicate he was not one of those men, Alex was separating himself from the bad guys in a very powerful nonverbal way. Whenever the problem of her old pain from a previous relationship came up, he dissociated himself from the old pain by anchoring it to something away from himself. Then he was able to use both negative and positive anchors to smooth out his relationship. Soon Stephanie began to see him in a new light, standing by himself, and not as one of the crowd of men who had treated her badly.

Another client of mine used negative anchoring to help his lover get over her fear of commitment. She had been married before to a man who she discovered was a child abuser. She was always watching to see if my client showed any signs of being interested in her sixteen-year-old daughter. My client was outraged. "She actually said I was looking at her daughter 'that way,'" he told me.

The next time he got a chance, he used negative anchoring by saying "Some men like young girls" and pointing to a corner of the room. "But most men like a mature woman they can talk to. A grown-up, like themselves," he continued, then pointing to himself.

It's important to separate yourself in your woman's eyes from all the other men she's ever known, especially from a man whose past bad behavior haunts her and keeps the two of you from being as close as you'd like. Everyone has a past, and sometimes it's hard to get over the old hurts. Using negative and positive anchoring, you can help the woman you love appreciate your good qualities while dissociating yourself from the bad feelings she has attached to other relationships.

Using Old Anchors

The woman you love already has positive and negative
anchors. We all do. Be sure to associate yourself with her
positive anchors. For instance, she may love her cat. If you
lean over and pet the cat, some of the love she has for the
cat will spill over onto you. If she loves her mother, then
sit next to her mother at the next family dinner to let
those loving feelings encompass you too.

On the other hand, suppose she hates her brother-in-
law. He's the guy to keep away from. If you're standing
next to him in the next family snapshot, some of her hate
may unconsciously spill over onto you every time she
looks at the picture. Positioning yourself in close proximity to the people, pets, and even inanimate objects she
loves (her piano, for instance) will let you enjoy the automatic spillover from her already-established love anchors.

No matter how difficult it may seem at first, try to like
her friends of both sexes. If you don't, she'll be suspicious.
You'll be in disagreement, but worst of all, you won't get
a chance to enjoy the love, trust, and friendship anchors
she's established with them.

CHAPTER TWELVE

Getting Her to Do What You Want in Bed

Tonight's the night. You're finally getting her into bed. You're hot and horny, ready for all-orifice, ten-digit sex—a real night to remember. But guess what? She recoils from your favorite foreplay, pulls you into the missionary position, and acts like she's doing you a favor.

Horrified, you think to yourself, "How could I have possibly gotten this far without knowing she's a prude? I mean, she *looks* so sexy. . . ."

Once upon a time, in the days of carefree, casual sex, people checked out their sexual compatibility before they exchanged last names. If she disappointed you in bed, you just "shined it on" and found a new bed partner. These days, disappointment in bed can follow a major investment of time in getting to know a woman. You may even be in love.

Even in today's new environment, you can avoid disappointment in bed. This involves two steps:

1. Finding out how sexy she really is—long before you go to bed with her.

2. Making sure she's really ready to go to bed with
   you.

Checking her out and assuring great sex start with getting some questions answered right away. Is she interested in sex? Is she hot? How can you find out as soon as possible so that you don't waste a lot of time with a sexually incompatible woman? If she seems uptight, can you loosen her up, or is she simply a lost cause?

So how do you know if she's hot or not? Here are some simple clues.

Signs of a Sexy Woman

She touches you a lot. She likes it when you touch her.
She wants to be close. She likes to kiss.
She isn't "body shy." She kisses with her whole body up
   against yours, pelvis to pelvis.
Her ex-lovers are always hanging around.
Sometimes she doesn't wear underwear.
She admires men's and women's bodies.
She loves a massage, whether sensual or therapeutic.
She's relaxed, warm, and giving.
Her gestures are expansive and open.
She thinks of ways to make you feel good.
She's willing to talk about sex.

As part of getting to know a new woman, discuss the general issues of morality and sexuality. Her willingness to discuss these issues, and her attitudes about them, will give you good clues to her sexuality. Ask whether she thinks sex should be taught in school and whether birth control or abortion should be available to teenagers, whether homosexuality is immoral, whether pornography should be a federal issue. Should nudist camps be allowed?

Should parents be open with their children about sex?
Should prostitution be legalized? If people could press a
button and have orgasms whenever they wanted, would
she have a button at her house?

If she answers on the conservative side of every question, you can be pretty sure she'll be sexually conservative. No ball of fire here. If she answers more on the liberal
side, then she's more likely to be sexually open. Also,
talking about general issues related to sex sets you up for
the next step.

Finding Out Ahead of Time Whether She Likes What You Like

Here's an amazingly effective secret for finding out what
she's likely to do in bed before you get her there. Make
sure that you're in a conversational setting and that the
timing doesn't make her feel threatened or cornered.
Then, in a casual way, ask her what she thinks most
women want in a lover. Never ask her what *she* wants in
bed, and be prepared to discuss what "most men want in
a lover."

The key to this approach is that it takes the personal
pressure off. She doesn't feel interrogated. By talking
about other people, she actually gets to talk about herself,
but not in an embarrassing way. Talking about sex is easier
if you're talking about other people. You can be sure that
what she says about "all women" is exactly what she likes.
We all think we're representative of our sex.

How to Make Sure She's Ready

It's best not to rush into bed until she's really ready. As
one man told me, "I never pick the fruit until it's falling

off the tree into my hand. If it's not ripe, it's hard and unyielding. When it's ripe, it's juicy and fragrant, succulent and sweet and bursting with flavor. There's no comparison."

Before even starting the seduction steps outlined below, you'll want to know that she's generally ready. By that I mean she's decided she wants you; it's just a question of when and how. Here's how you can tell that "the fruit is ripening."

She's starting to "slip into something comfortable" (and revealing) after she invites you in for a nightcap.

You're very relaxed together when discussing sex, the discussions have gotten frank and explicit, and you've finally gotten personal about the issues of monogamy and safe sex.

But even if making love is a foregone conclusion, you don't want to skip the seduction.

Seduction

Seduction starts when you're not there. It begins with anticipation. You can up the anticipation level by getting her excited on the phone or in a note. Tell her how beautiful you think she is, how much you're looking forward to being with her.

Seduction continues all the time you're together, starting when you show up and mirror her. Getting into agreement with her is seductive. So don't argue, don't disagree, don't bring up problems. Tell her how sexy she is.

When you take her out to eat, showing your ability to give and provide, you're being subtly seductive. Keep telling her how lovely she is, and how crazy you are about her. Be sure it's a totally romantic evening, one that builds steadily toward lovemaking.

After you're back at her place, or your place, all the advice for first-time lovemaking can be summed up in three little words: *Take your time.*

How to Ask For What You Want and Get It

Never ask for anything in anger.
Always say three nice things first.
Don't ask for it when you're in bed or about to go to bed.
Ask in a nonsexual, noncontroversial, relaxed situation.
Mirror first. Be sure you're in tune with her.
Don't criticize. Instead of saying, "I don't like it when you . . . ," say, "I would love it if you would . . ."
Hold hands, put your arm around her, be sure you're touching when you ask.
Find a way to make it in her interest to do what you want.
You could say, "It would turn me on so much if you would . . ." Or "I've never been able to resist a woman who . . ." Or "If a woman ever did that for me, I'd be her slave for life."

However, you've got to be realistic. You're not going to turn a prissy princess into a lusty lady by asking nicely. The idea is to avoid being that far off target to begin with.

Even with the best groundwork, though, you can wind up in love with a woman who seems somewhat incompatible. Jack was in that situation when he and Sally came to me for help. They had been together only a year, but their sex life was just getting worse. Jack said he loved Sally, but he wasn't happy with her in bed. Jack loved Sally's sweetness and her gentle, kind ways, but he yearned for hotter, more satisfying sex.

Sally was upset too. She didn't quite understand why Jack was so unhappy with her. "I do everything he wants," she said. "I just don't get it."

Jack, for his part, was feeling guilty. He was beginning to spend a lot of time daydreaming about women he'd known in the past whose personality didn't please him as much as Sally's but with whom he'd had a very lusty sex life.

Jack wanted Sally to be more aggressive in bed, to initiate sex sometimes, but he didn't want to tell her what he wanted. He would talk in circles about her being more outgoing or her not really enjoying sex with him, which she vehemently denied.

"If she really loved me," Jack insisted, "she would just want to do it. I wouldn't have to prompt her." He felt that sex should come naturally. Besides, he felt that his prompting her would really mean that she was being aggressive only because he was forcing her to. "That takes the fun out of it," he complained. "I want her to think of it by herself."

Sally became depressed and unhappy, which made Jack even more upset with her. Sally felt that her femininity and sexuality were being questioned, and she was afraid that Jack was going to leave her. In this state of mind, she obviously didn't feel like being more aggressive; in fact, she felt inadequate and became more withdrawn. Sally and Jack had hit a serious stalemate.

In order to get Sally to do what he wanted, Jack had to give up the fantasy that she would do it spontaneously: In general, it was against her sweet, passive nature to be aggressive in bed. Besides, Jack really liked her demure personality. Jack learned that for Sally to be happy and responsive in bed he had to stop criticizing her. Instead, he started praising what she did do, to encourage her to do more.

Jack began to realize, too, that his unreasonable demand for a sweet, passive, gentle woman who was very aggressive sexually was a way for him to avoid commitment, since he could never find the impossible.

If a woman is passive and tractable out of bed, it's unreasonable to expect her to become a tiger in the bedroom. Conversely, if a woman is aggressive in bed, it's unreasonable to expect her to become a sweet, passive flower out of the bedroom.

When What You Want Is "Different"

You love her, but you have this uncontrollable desire to live out a sexual fantasy that embarrasses you more than a little. Your ex used to love it when you tied her up and the two of you played out sexual fantasies that involved bondage and spanking. Only you're afraid to tell the new woman in your life about your secret sexual fantasy. On the other hand, you know you'll never be really satisfied unless you get her in on it.

This is not something you bring up on the first date, or the second. Esoteric sex practices can scare a woman off if she doesn't have a chance to get to know and trust you first. If you've been dating her for some time and you've been mirroring her and developing trust, you'll have a better chance of having her accept your quirky sex practices and become involved in them.

Never demand that a woman participate in any sex act. It will just make her more determined not to do it, or if she feels coerced and does do it, she'll be predisposed not to like it.

When bringing up the subject of a new and different sex act, it's best to approach the subject sideways rather than directly. The best way to begin is to let your early, exploratory discussions of sex (see above) drift into the general subject of fantasies. Then arrange for both of you to read one or two books on the subject, which you can then discuss together.

For this purpose, I recommend starting with books like *My Secret Garden* or *Pleasures,* which go into a wide variety of fantasies. (Be careful about *The Story of O.* You may have heard that it's a classic. It is, but it involves heavy-duty S&M—not ideal introductory fare.)

You will be able to tell a lot from her initial reaction to a book like *My Secret Garden.* Lead her into the discussion gently, with a mildly positive remark like "Pretty trippy stuff. I guess most guys have a lot of those fantasies. Do you think most women do too?" (The book has already told her they do.) Watch her body language carefully. A little nervousness is normal. But do her eyes narrow, does her brow furrow, does she pull away from you? If so, you may have a real problem introducing this lady to any exotic sex.

Hopefully, she will gradually feel comfortable discussing other people's fantasies with you. This tells you she has become "desensitized" to the subject. Then you can ask for her reaction to something she's read concerning your particular sexual desires—but indirectly, never pushing her to answer for herself. "This rape fantasy—they say even feminists have this a lot. Do you think that's true?" Always talk about others rather than about yourselves, until she has let you know that she's really turned on by one fantasy or another.

After you get over the initial barrier and are able to talk freely about exotic sex acts, she'll feel less anxiety about the subject. As you talk, you'll both begin to feel closer, and she'll feel safer. Soon you'll feel comfortable talking about your most secret sex fantasies.

When you finally do confess your secret desires, do it in a conspiratorial, rather than a demanding, way. The more you tell the woman you love about your sexuality (starting in small doses in the beginning, but revealing more as you get closer), the more she'll tell you about hers. You'll be amazed how easily you can share secrets you've never told before.

One way to tell your new woman about a particular sexual fantasy of yours, especially if it's unusual, is through magazines. No matter what you like, there is a magazine about it. From sex with an amputee to bondage and discipline, your local erotic newsstand has it all. If you fantasize about a sex act that you can't find represented at an X-rated newsstand or bookstore, it's probably so illegal you shouldn't be doing it anyway.

Then, when the two of you are relaxing, at a no-sexual-pressure time (that means you don't expect her to go right to bed and perform), show her the magazines. Discuss the photographs with her as if you were doing a critique or study, not as if you wanted to throw her down and do those things yourself. Tell her which photographs you think are a turn-on and which you don't think are very erotic. Ask her which ones she thinks are sexy.

Having a couple of magazines or books that include your fantasy gives it some credibility in her eyes and gets you off the weirdo hook. At least she'll know you're not the only man in the world who likes to wear women's underwear or tie up his loved one.

By talking about sex in a no-pressure situation, you will become more open about other parts of your life as well. When one person is candid, it encourages openness in the other. The time to convince her to do something you want is not when you hit the bedroom; it's way before. The bedroom is no place to debate issues. When you're in bed, make love, not war.

The next time you want your lover to do something special, don't just push her hand or maneuver her into position. Use books, movies, or magazines to stimulate conversation and discussion, and begin by generalizing about what other people like. Discuss sex outside of bed; then it's easier to do what you want *in* bed. Sharing your intimate secrets with a woman is a sign to her that you trust her. Should she become upset with you about what you tell her, you might want to remind her that you only told her because you trust her and have faith that your relationship can be based on truth. Just be careful not to share too much too soon.

Sexual Teasing

Suppose your woman has confessed to you that she fantasizes about being made love to by two men at once. Instead of getting upset about her fantasy, you can include it in some light sexual teasing. Sexual teasing is one way of arousing a woman even before you get to the bedroom. And knowing your partner's sexual fantasies can be a big help.

You're standing in line at the movies or at the buffet table with your woman, who has confessed that she likes being spanked during sex. "You've been a really bad girl tonight," you whisper in her ear, "and when I get you home, I'm going to spank your bottom." She looks surprised, because the sex talk is out of context and unexpected—but you've started her thinking about the two of you in bed later. You've excited her in a public place with talk of illicit sex, which is almost like necking in an elevator or making love on the kitchen table. It's exciting because it's a like a naughty secret shared between the two of you.

A woman feels freer with a fantasy if there's no expectation that she act it out right then. She feels less threatened by a sex fantasy whispered in a movie line because there's no immediate pressure to perform. She can let her imagination run wild, and her excitement will carry over into the bedroom later.

Talk to her in the supermarket about your fantasies, or on your way to the theater or out to dinner. Bring the subject up and let her imagine the two of you doing it later.

Be light; don't get too heavy. Don't make her feel obligated. Use a teasing tone of voice. And don't do it all the time. Once in a while is enough. Plant the idea and give it time to gel in her mind. Give her a chance to picture the two of you doing it and to imagine how it would feel. Then, when the actual time comes, she'll be much less hesitant about becoming involved in an unusual sex act. It won't seem strange or unusual to her anymore because she's already played it out in her mind.

Turning Her On With "Method Sex"

You're hot and she's not. It happens, even among the best of couples. You've wined her and dined her, praised and complimented her, mirrored and anchored her, and you can tell she loves you. She just doesn't feel like sex. She's not in the mood.

You're not to blame, but somehow you feel as though you've failed, as though there were something wrong with you. You feel rejected. But you are not being rejected. Sex is being rejected. If she doesn't feel like having sex with you, it doesn't mean she doesn't want or love you; it simply means she's not mentally in the mood.

You wonder whether you've said the wrong thing or inadvertently turned her off without even knowing it. But you didn't turn her off. She did. The turn-on, turn-off switch is in her mind, not yours. Maybe her mind was on a big project she hasn't finished, or maybe somebody rejected her work, or maybe she got bad news.

Before trying to turn her on, be sure that nothing really serious has happened, like a death in the family. Mirror her, and use her love language to draw her out about the problem. If it's not serious, if it's something she'd rather put out of her mind anyway, there's a simple technique you can use to turn her back on—a special anchoring technique I call "method sex."

In method sex you turn her on the same way method actors get into the mood to play a scene—by remembering similar feelings from their past. When method actors get in touch with the feelings or the memory anchor from their past, they are not just acting, they are actually reliving their own experiences. Then they draw on that emotion and put it in the scene they are currently playing.

By getting your woman to remember a past sexual experience, her sexual feelings will be stimulated no matter what else she's feeling. Ask her if she can remember her most romantic or most erotic experience.

She probably won't want to jump right in and tell you all about it. If she's in a really bad mood, she may even be annoyed that you asked. That's okay. Reassure her that you're not asking her to name names or get into graphic detail. Just be gently persistent; ask her to describe the place where she and her friend made love, when it was, what they had been doing before.

Ask questions all around the sex act, but not directly about the sex act itself. That way you won't embarrass her, and yet as she tells you about the essential nonsexual details, the sexual ones will also be running through her mind. She'll be remembering exactly what happened and she'll also be remembering the feelings she had.

As she recalls the past, watch the expression on her face. Is there an easing of tension around the mouth and eyes? Perhaps a slight smile? Does she seem to be slipping into a good memory? If so, this is an ideal time to note your lover's "in lust" expression. File it away so that you'll always know when she's aroused, even if there are no signs except the expression on her face.

Also, the minute you see signs that she's remembering an exciting sexual experience from her past, anchor her sexy feeling and the memory of when she was so aroused.

Touch her hand or the back of her neck, or use any of the other anchoring techniques. In this way she'll transfer some of her sexy feelings from the past to you, and you can set up an "in lust" anchor that you can use whenever you want. Soon you'll be able to get her to recall the sexual feeling without remembering the past sex experience at all. She'll just recall the feeling.

Strengthen your sex anchor by adding to it. Say something in her love language that puts you in agreement with her. If she's a visual woman, touch her and say, "I can see why that was exciting for you." If she's an auditory woman, say, "I can hear how thrilling that was for you." If she's a feelings woman, say, "I understand how that excited you."

If she tells you about her past, you gain one more advantage. Not only do you know exactly what has turned her on in the past, but you can recreate the essence of that turn-on when you make love to her. If she tells you she was most turned on by making love in an unusual place or under an unusual circumstance, then you can try that. If it's a special kind of sex act, then try that. Get her to be as specific as possible so that you can duplicate that peak excitement. Don't worry about copying some other guy's technique. Just use it as a leg up, and then you can go on from there.

You can create different moods by finding out her different past anchors and transferring them to you. In the same way that recalling past sex experiences puts her in the mood for sex, recalling past love experiences can put her in the mood for love, right now, with you.

Ask her about the first time she fell in love. Watch her features soften as she looks at you and remembers how love feels. See how quickly and easily you are able to break down her barriers to intimacy by using her already established love anchors.

CHAPTER THIRTEEN

How Much to Give and How Soon

"I would give her anything she wants, but it just doesn't seem to do any good. She takes my presents, thanks me, tells me I'm a nice guy, but she doesn't love me." It's a story I've heard over and over again from men. He gives, gives, gives. She takes, takes, takes. And the other guy gets the girl.

Often, a man falls for a woman and feels compelled to give her everything—his heart, his soul, his love, his money. Sometimes men will deliberately attempt to buy love while avoiding intimacy, thinking that presents will make up for an inability or unwillingness to get close.

Most often, though, giving too much too soon is misguided hopefulness. "If I give enough, she'll have to give something back. That's only fair." Only it doesn't work that way. Love is not fair. This is not a tit-for-tat situation where you give so much and get so much back.

It's simplistic to think that by giving someone everything they're going to love you. Selective giving of a thoughtful nature is the kind of giving that counts, not just giving to get something back.

Ten Fatal Relationship Errors

FATAL RELATIONSHIP ERROR #1: GIVING TOO MUCH
TOO SOON

The biggest problem created by giving too much too soon
is that there's nothing left to discover. A woman loses
interest if you give everything right away. Knowing
there's a mysterious part of you that you haven't yet
shared keeps a woman interested.

The next problem with giving too much too soon is that
you look too easy, too desperate. You hardly know her,
and already you've given or offered her everything. You
think that's flattering, but what does she think?

She figures if you're that easy to get, any woman could
get you. She loses the feeling that she's special, that she's
the only woman in the world you'd give so much of yourself to, that nobody else but her is worthy.

Remember, all women want to feel special. That's why
it's so hard for a man to have more than one woman in his
life on a regular basis. Even if he were able to give enough
love, attention, and money to each woman, they wouldn't
be satisfied. None would feel special enough.

Put off giving expensive gifts as long as possible. For her
birthday, buy something somewhat special but without
obvious monetary value. Giving expensive gifts too soon
makes you look like a needy man who is trying to be
impressive, who is trying to buy love.

When you bring the element of money into a relationship, you put pressure on the woman. She may feel obligated to reciprocate with equally expensive gifts. Or she
may misread your intentions and think you see the relationship as transactional, gifts for sex. Or, rather than
being bothered by the gifts, she may come to expect an
ongoing flow of them from you and be very disappointed
if they're not forthcoming.

Some of the very best, the nicest, the smartest, and the most loving men have been left for giving too much too soon. They give too much of themselves before the appropriate time. They spend too much time with a woman, too much money on her—and she *knows* it's inappropriate giving.

Then, just to see if he'll still give so much, the woman does something slightly ungracious. She cuts him short on the phone or breaks a date. And what does he do? Does he tell her off, yell at her, even cut back on the invitations, gifts, and goodies? Oh, no. He just gives more to see if he can win back her attention. Naturally she thinks, "This is some kind of schmuck," and either drops or uses him, which leaves him feeling awful.

FATAL RELATIONSHIP ERROR #2: TELLING ABOUT HAVING BEEN A VICTIM

One way both men and women get in trouble in relationships is by telling too much about themselves too soon. When you meet someone new that you like, don't tell bad things about yourself. Present your best side. After all, you're competing with people who are showing only their best.

Never tell how some other woman did you wrong. Why give a new woman the wrong idea?

Never tell about how your ex took you. The new woman will only wonder why your ex hated you so much.

Don't tell a new woman how your mother or father mistreated you or how you can't get along with your family. She'll only think, "He must really be a case if his own family doesn't want anything to do with him."

The best policy is to tell as little as possible about yourself, especially if it's unflattering. Even flattering information should be doled out in small doses. A woman wants to keep finding out new and exciting things about the man she's getting involved with. It's important that you save little tidbits to give her, such as "Oh, yes, I won the wrestling championship at my college" or "I was chairman of our board of directors for the last three years." She needs to feel justified in her selection of you. Dropping wonderful little accomplishments every once in a while makes her feel reassured.

Telling everything about yourself in the beginning of a relationship ruins part of the romantic mystique. Remember Brenda Starr—how she loved the man with the black eye patch. That was because he was a mystery, because she was able to fantasize about him, and because she found out wonderful, endearing little tidbits about him as the relationship progressed. But she never found out everything, and that's what really kept her interested. Curiosity and mystery kept her romantic fantasy alive.

When you're talking to a new woman, don't just babble on and on about yourself. Babbling on may cause you to say the one thing that would kill your chances with her. Some things are best kept to yourself.

Never tell a new woman how you took advantage of another woman. She'll instantly put up her guard, wondering how you're trying to take advantage of her.

Try talking to a new woman about the things that interest her—her job, her life, her family, her vacations, her hobbies. If she's interested in crystals or computers, past lives therapy or archaeology, even shopping or needlepoint, talk about those things. Don't insist on talking only about the masculine pursuits that interest you.

By being open and interested in what *she* cares about, you'll set yourself apart from all the other men, who are interested only in cars, sports, and business. She'll conclude that you'll be sensitive, flexible, and open to lots of new ideas, and she'll share more and more of herself with you.

FATAL RELATIONSHIP ERROR #3: BEING TOO MUCH OF A GOOD GUY

Some men make the fatal mistake of trying to be the perfect "Good Guy"—to do everything, to be so nice they're irresistible. Unfortunately, some women haven't learned to appreciate good guys. There's something sexy about a man who's intractable, a bit stubborn, hard to capture, not too free with his gifts or his love. He's the prize, the guy all women want, the one who's hard to get, the one not just any woman can have.

The perfect "Good Guy" never gets the girl. Often he doesn't even get sex, but he still hangs around, because after all, he's so good he's not demanding. He just loves purely, without getting anything back. His is the kind of love that is doomed to suffer.

The good guy doesn't necessarily give money or gifts, but he always gives so much of his time, so much of himself, that he actually scares women off.

In the beginning of a relationship you are not supposed to get her car fixed, baby-sit her kids, do her shopping, and, in general, "be there" for her.

FATAL RELATIONSHIP ERROR #4: ALWAYS BEING THERE

In order to feel in love, a woman needs a chance to fantasize about you. If you are there all the time, if she already knows everything about you, there is nothing to fantasize about. She can't imagine how you're spending your time. She already knows. She can't daydream about you or what you might do. You're already there doing it.

The beginning of a relationship should take place slowly.

FATAL RELATIONSHIP ERROR #5: STARTING OUT ON TOO HIGH A ROMANTIC NOTE

Almost everyone has had a relationship in which you start out hot and heavy, and then something happens—you're not sure what—and it's over. Rarely does anybody figure out why.

Sometimes you can't help yourself. You say "I love you" too soon. It slips out of your mouth before you know what you're doing. Those three little words are in the air. If you're lucky, she says them back, and then you say them again, and she says them again. Soon you are calling each other three times a day saying "I love you." You start sending cute cards and notes and soon you're spending every evening together.

Then, just once, you get tied up and forget to call and she thinks, "Oops, that's it, it's the end. He forgot to call." And so she doesn't call, and you think, "Whoops, that's it." When you do talk, each of you is waiting for the other to say "I love you." When you finally say it, she responds halfheartedly, and the relationship is over almost as quickly as it began.

FATAL RELATIONSHIP ERROR #6: APPEARING NEEDY

Since a woman is often looking for a man who will be a good provider, nothing turns her off faster than a needy man. Looking for a good provider may not be her primary concern in finding a man, but you can believe it will be right up there—either consciously or subconsciously.

Being needy doesn't just mean you appear to be a poor provider monetarily. It also means you appear to be a poor provider of emotional, spiritual, and psychological support—all those things a woman wants.

Men and women often ask me if they should let someone think they're dating other people. The answer is yes,
of course. If you had a new business and you had only one
client, would you let that client know? Of course not.
Neither should you let a woman know she is the only
woman you are seeing—and she shouldn't be.

If a woman thinks she is the only woman you are seeing,
she immediately thinks nobody else wants you. Then her
next thought is "Maybe, if nobody else wants him, he's no
great prize." Women are competitive. For a woman, winning often means getting the best man, so it's important
that other women want you too. That way, when she gets
you, she'll feel as if she has won an important prize away
from lots of other women. Rather like winning a beauty
pageant.

The best way to avoid appearing needy is to be unavail-
able, to play hard to get. But instead of *playing* hard to
get, *be* hard to get. The more fun you have without her,
the more she'll want to be with you.

FATAL RELATIONSHIP ERROR #7: CALLING TOO OFTEN

When you call a woman too often, especially in the beginning of a relationship, she thinks you're too easy, too
eager. You become a pest, not a pleasure. She figures she
has you all wrapped up, so she can stop trying. After all,
she's already got more of you than she needs.

Practice not calling her for a day or two. Call sporadically, on no set schedule. It's the intermittent calls that
make a woman yearn to hear from you.

RELATIONSHIP ERROR #8: LETTING HER GET
AWAY WITH THINGS IN THE BEGINNING OF THE
RELATIONSHIP SO THAT SHE LEARNS TO TREAT YOU
BADLY

When a woman gets away with being late, flirting with
other men, putting you down, standing you up, lying, or
anything else she shouldn't do, she begins to think less of
you. After all, what kind of a man would put up with that
kind of behavior?

The time to make a stand is in the beginning, before
you're in love and before you've invested too much in the
relationship. If you don't put your foot down right away,
she'll not only think you're a wimp but wonder what else
you'll let her get away with. By saying nothing, you teach
her to treat you badly.

Another problem: She begins to get a thrill from having gotten away with something. Then she gets to like
the thrill and wants it more often. Find other ways to
give her thrills. Don't let her get them from walking all
over you.

FATAL RELATIONSHIP ERROR #9: INTRODUCING HER
TO FRIENDS AND FAMILY TOO SOON

In cave man days, it was the woman who had to leave her
tribe and go to the man's tribe, where she had to fit in. The
man's relatives and friends were always a little unwelcom-
ing and suspicious. They had a show-me attitude.

Some things never change. When you bring a woman
into your circle of friends and relatives, there will be some
people who are afraid of losing their access to you, who
want you all to themselves, who don't want to share you
at all. There will be others who want to make sure you're
not making a mistake and bringing home a shrew.

They're going to be looking her over carefully, watching for the first mistake, and she knows it.

Bringing a woman home to meet your family and friends is a high-anxiety situation. Put it off as long as possible. That way, you have time to build a firm base before your friends and relatives get into the act, telling you that you deserve better, that she's not good enough, that you ought to have a movie star who cooks like Betty Crocker and keeps house like Heloise. Remember, it's you who has to live with her, not your mother or your friends.

FATAL RELATIONSHIP ERROR #10: TRYING AGAIN

Once a relationship is on a downward spiral, it's almost impossible to turn it around. The advice in this book works best for new relationships, where you haven't set any bad precedents. In other words, you haven't let her walk all over you, or done or said anything crazy.

Even though it's almost impossible to set an old relationship straight, if you insist on trying, here's how. Stay away from the woman for a while. No communication, no seeing each other. For about six weeks, act as if you've fallen in love with someone else. Then, when you get back together, try treating the relationship like a new one.

It's hard to set an old relationship straight—to avoid bringing up old angers and indiscretions, to forget how you've hurt each other, to learn new ways of relating. Another problem with trying again: When you're busy trying to fix problems in the old relationship, you may not see opportunities with new people. You're not really a free agent, and women sense it. If you're hung up on an old love, it probably won't work out anyway and you'll miss out on a new one. It's always easier to start with someone new.

When Overgiving Starts

How do you know you've given too much too soon? Simple. You feel bad. You feel cheated. When you've given too much too soon, you expect a lot back. When you don't get it, you start to feel like a jerk. So you try harder and give more, wondering what's wrong with you and how come she doesn't give you anything back. Maybe you think you haven't given enough. You're anxious and worried all the time. All your giving makes her uncomfortable; she knows she's not going to keep up, and she starts to pull away. Again you give more, and she doesn't respond. After all, why should she? She's already learned she doesn't have to give anything in return to keep you giving.

Why You Overgive

Overgiving stems from insecurity. You think that a woman won't like you just because you're you, so you start figuring out ways to endear yourself to her. Only you overdo it. You wind up appearing exactly the way you are, insecure.

A secure man doesn't have to call every five minutes or date a woman up for every Saturday night ahead for the next two years. He doesn't have to keep sending cute little cards or bouquets of flowers to remind her that he exists. He doesn't have to shower her with gifts. He feels secure that she'll be thinking of him. He feels that he is valuable and unique, that there is no other man in the world just like him. He feels able to give enough in lasting human qualities—caring, affection, support, and compassion—that she will love him for himself.

Overgiving is also a symptom of low self-esteem. Raising the value on yourself is the cure. It's also the way to show another person you're lovable. Who would love someone who doesn't value himself? Nobody you'd want.

If low self-esteem is your problem, try reprogramming your brain with positive affirmations: "I am lovable, I am wonderful," etc. You might also want to use negative conditioning for the thoughts that poison your psyche and lead to low self-esteem. When you start to tell yourself you're not handsome enough, rich enough, lovable enough, or whatever, pinch yourself or zap yourself with a rubber band. Punish your own bad mental behavior. Reward your good behavior.

When you don't like yourself, it's hard for others to like you. Women all report liking men who are at ease with themselves, who have a good sense of self-worth.

When to Say "I Love You"

Important laboratory-proven love theory: In order to have the in-love feeling, a woman must have her love returned somewhat, but not altogether. Yet she must have hope of having that love returned altogether at some time in the future.

The best way to give a woman the in-love feeling is to give her some quality time—some real attention—but less than she wants, and on an intermittent schedule so that she's always yearning for more.

It's usually best to let the woman say "I love you" first. That way you have the love advantage. But you should always say it after she does. Never say "I love you" more than she does at the beginning of the relationship. After you're committed, it's okay. It's also okay if you slip and say "I love you" in a moment of uncontrollable passion, but serious "I love you"s should never be overdone at first or they lose their meaning.

First Aid for Overgivers

Everybody makes mistakes. You may have already made
the mistake of overgiving. You may have let "I love you"
slip out too soon too many times. You may have called too
often, or blurted out something really stupid like "I'm not
seeing anyone else" before she does, or given an overly
expensive gift. You *know* you've given too much too soon
because you feel unrewarded and deprived, and the
woman of your dreams is starting to pull away. She senses
your faux pas.

Getting Her Back

If you have already gone overboard, there is no easy way
to recover. As I've advised earlier, it's usually easier to
start a new relationship the right way than to try to fix one
that's off to a bad start. But if you are determined to make
a salvage attempt, all you can do is back off the relationship immediately.

Back off further than she already has. It's tough medicine, but it's the only cure. Make yourself scarce. Go fish-
ing with your buddies. Go visit your parents or some old
friends. Throw yourself into your work and don't take any
calls. Keep your telephone answering machine on. Force
her to keep calling if she wants to know what has happened to you.

You must give her a chance to miss you and to fantasize
about you. You have to make her worry about losing you
to someone else. How can she worry about losing you if
you're either right there or she knows you're mooning
about her?

The Importance of Fantasizing

Proven love theory: Fantasizing about the love object is one of the most important ingredients of love.

When a man or woman is in love, he or she tends to fantasize about the loved one. A woman fantasizes about how wonderful the man is. She daydreams about him, and in her mind he becomes a knight in shining armor—better-looking, smarter, braver, more interesting, and more exciting than any other man in the world. Then she decides she wants to be with him forever because he's so wonderful.

When people say love is blind, what they're really talking about is this tendency to fantasize, to aggrandize the love object. You've certainly heard a woman talking about the man she loves. If you know the guy, her description sounds like that of a different person. Even the worst scoundrel, the biggest jerk, sounds terrific when a woman in love tells about him. She thinks he's a prince, of course. She'll tell you how brilliant he is (and you know he's not that bright), or how kind and affectionate and giving he is (and you know he's a selfish son of a bitch).

That's part of falling in love. You have to be convinced that the other person is the most wonderful person in the world. If you want a woman to fall in love with you, give her time to fantasize about how wonderful you are.

So if you've overgiven, go away. She may date other men while you're gone, but she'll be comparing the real them to the fantasy you. You'll have a decent chance of coming out ahead because fantasies are always better than reality.

The withdrawal tactic is risky, but you really have no other choice. If you're in a relationship that's getting worse because you've given too much too soon, you may already have blown it. If withdrawal works and she comes back, you have a second chance to try relating without overgiving. If the relationship still doesn't work, at least you didn't give any more.

When to Cut Your Losses

If she comes back to you after you've made yourself scarce, but she still hasn't changed her taking ways, then it's definitely time to cut your losses. You've already lost her anyway, but that won't make you feel any better about it.

In fact, you'll probably feel worse because now you know for sure she didn't want you, she only wanted all that extra giving. So now you feel awful about yourself, you don't have a girlfriend, and you can't get one because nobody wants a guy who doesn't feel good about himself.

While you're feeling that way, the only woman you'll find is a woman with low self-esteem just like you. But the problem there is that no matter how much you love each other, you'll have a hard time convincing each other that you do. This is because people with low self-esteem don't really believe they're lovable, so they have trouble accepting love. That's the real downside of giving too much too soon.

Don't let the problem get that far. If you find yourself with an indifferent woman and suspect that you've given too much too soon, cut the relationship off cold. No more phone calls, no returning or retrieving of belongings. Don't waste your valuable time on a woman who doesn't want you, especially now that you have the power to create a truly loving relationship right from the start. So begin seeing other women right away.

This time, don't give too much too soon. No gifts. No money. No showing off how much you have to give. No saying "I love you" before she does just to force her hand. No volunteering to forsake all others before she's ready to do the same.

But there are ways to set up an atmosphere where she'll want to be yours and yours alone.

Why Indifference Works

Have you ever noticed the guy who treats women with a little indifference and has them crawling all over him? His phone never stops ringing. He has to beat them off with a stick. The reason is that every so often, out of boredom or pity, the indifferent man gives some attention to a woman he doesn't care that much for. Those little dribs and drabs of attention keep her hooked. Just that much is all it takes. Too much is like overwatering a plant. It drowns.

The little drops of niceness you give out to someone who doesn't interest you can make her crazy with love for you. Acting indifferent is easy when you don't care. The hard part is acting a little indifferent when you *do* care a lot.

When you see the woman you want, the natural male urge is to drag her back to your place, declare your love, be totally honest, let all your feelings hang out, and let her see everything about you. Don't do it. You'll just scare her away.

Of course, indifference works on you too. Have you ever wondered why the women you don't really care about are so available and the ones you want so badly make themselves scarce? If a woman acts indifferent toward you, your natural inclination may be to try harder to see if you can please her. To give more. But the way to make her stop acting indifferent is to act even more indifferent than she does.

Sticking to a plan in relationships is hard because we all want to throw caution to the wind when we fall in love and let our emotions lead the way. Unfortunately, that's exactly the wrong thing to do. If you've had trouble with relationships, learning how much to give and how soon can mean the difference between success and failure.

When to Give Your All

When you feel as if she's giving her all to you, then you give your all to her. When you have both made a mutual commitment to each other, then you can be almost totally giving.

But never give everything. No matter how much you give, you are always entitled to a private part of you that's just for you—your core. That's the part you should never give away. It may be only 10 percent that you keep tucked away, but it's all yours. Treasure it.

CHAPTER FOURTEEN

Assuring Return Engagements

To make a woman fall in love with you, you must create a desire in her to see you over and over again. Her fantasy may be that you do all the pursuing, all the asking, all the planning, taking, and doing, but that's not good for you. You don't want to be the one who's always calling and asking for time together, the one who is totally responsible for getting the two of you together. You want her to call you. You want her to want you, all the time, especially when you're not there. You want her to yearn for you, to desire you, to need you.

By now, of course, you've noticed that the woman you desire never calls, while the women you could easily live without call all the time. Some women are just stuck in the old-fashioned "He has to call" mindset. Others won't call because they're afraid you'll think they're desperate. In this chapter you're going to learn how to inspire the right woman to want you, to call you, to need to be with you.

Last-Minute Dates

Waiting until the last minute to call for a date is the wrong way to make a woman want you. Occasionally, a spontaneous, last-minute call is legitimate. "I've just gotten a promotion and I'd love you to have a drink and celebrate with me" might work for afternoon cocktails, but don't assume she's free for the rest of the evening. "I just got a new car and I'd love to take you for a ride" is a little more suspect—I mean, didn't you know ahead of time you were going to pick up the car? That one might sound legit, but only if it's Saturday afternoon.

Even though promotions and new cars don't happen every week, guys are forever calling women on the spur of the moment, hoping to pop right over and get laid. Some of the lines are pretty transparent, including the routine where you call and say, "I just got a bottle of vintage Château LaFitte and I'd love to share it with you tonight." Or "I've been thinking all day about how sexy you are. Are you busy tonight?"

All of the above may or may not work, for several reasons. She may turn you down just on general principles, because you called so late. She may think you're being cheap and want to get laid without taking her out on a full-fledged date. She may think you want only quickies and not a full relationship with her. She may have other plans. Or she just may be horny and decide, "What the hell? Why not?"

Either way, calling at the eleventh hour is insulting to her. If she accepts an obvious last-minute offer, she won't feel good about herself or you later on. If she doesn't accept, she'll figure that you'll just keep calling other women until you find one who's desperate enough to say yes, and that won't leave her with a very complimentary picture of you or who you're willing to go to bed with.

In any event, you don't want her to get in the habit of

saying no to you. You want her to get in the habit of
saying yes to you, so don't set yourself up for a turn-
down by calling with a last-minute offer. You'll sound a
little desperate to begin with, and if she turns you down,
you'll sound even worse. It's hard to sound suave at 6
P.M. when you've just been turned down for that evening.

Sometimes a man will go to great lengths to see a
woman whether she wants to see him or not. One very old
ploy is to volunteer to fix something for her and then
"accidentally" leave behind your power drill, which you
absolutely must have two days later. Surely no woman
would be so cold as to deny you the return of your needed
drill, especially when you left it while fixing something for
her. The problem is that the woman often knows exactly
what's going on, and your image suddenly changes from
cute handyman to hard-up pest.

Worse yet, the whole ploy can backfire and you can lose
both your tools and your woman. A client of mine lent a
woman an expensive Nikon camera with an automatic
zoom lens for her trip abroad. She came back with a fiancé
she'd met in Europe and told my client she'd lost the
camera. He always suspected that she'd given it to her
new fiancé.

Some men give women gifts such as flowers or candy or
perfume in the hope that they'll be remembered when
she looks at the flowers, eats the candy, or dabs the perfume behind her ear. She will think of you, but there's no
assurance she won't share the candy with, or wear the
perfume for, some other guy. She could even use your
flowers to make him jealous.

There's nothing wrong with giving a woman presents if
she's giving you something back. But if there's a one-way
stream of gifts from you to her with nothing coming back,
you're setting yourself up for trouble.

Gifts can mean a lot to women. Even a little trinket can

signify that you care for her. Actually, the best gifts are thoughtful but not costly, because you don't want to put a monetary value on the relationship.

Some gifts are just gifts; others do double duty and function as "memory triggers." An effective memory trigger makes her think of you and yearn to be with you. A gift that acts as a memory trigger can even stimulate her to call you, to arrange to take you out on dates, and to buy you presents too.

One of the first gifts my husband gave me when we started dating was a personalized license plate for my car that read GR8 WRTR (for Great Writer). Clever man. Every day, every time I went anywhere in the car, there was his love trigger working away on me.

Subtle Love Triggers

You don't have to give her anything in order to trigger a romantic memory of you. Consider your after-shave. For years, knowing women have sprayed little doses of their perfume on a man's pillows, to subtly remind him of themselves after they're gone. Your after-shave will work just as well. She smells it and thinks of you. Or you leave your special brand of toothpaste in the bathroom, or a special soap or shampoo in the shower. She washes with it and thinks of you.

Once you know your woman's love language, the subtle love triggers you choose to remind her of you when you're not around can be directly related to her love language. When you choose a directly related trigger, it will be even more effective.

If you have a visual lover, you'll want to leave something around that will stimulate her sense of sight—for instance, a beautiful coffee-table book you picked out just for her about a subject that interests her. Whenever she looks at it, she will think of you. Another visually stimulating love trigger might be a photograph of the two of you when you had a particularly romantic time together or when she was especially happy. Not only does she think of you, but she remembers how much fun the two of you can have together. Another visual trigger might be a plant or a dried-flower arrangment.

Never give something too big or too gaudy. Make sure that any gift fits with her decor and that she'll like it. If you have any doubt, don't give anything. Looking at something she hates wouldn't add to her loving feelings toward you; it would only serve as a reminder that you really don't understand her.

If you're in love with an auditory woman, give her something that sounds nice—a set of lovely wind chimes, musical bells for her phone, a favorite record or CD. Try to think of something she'll hear all the time that will remind her of you. Never give her anything that makes a racket.

Love triggers for feelings women are easy. Try some special bubble bath that the two of you enjoy together, a wonderful scented massage oil that you rub on her, or a silky scarf—anything that feels good and can trigger a sexual memory. Candy is dandy, but it's soon gone. Besides, lots of women are on diets, so they may even resent you for giving it to them.

Should you think of a wonderfully appropriate love trigger that isn't in your woman's love language, use it anyway. Every woman has a primary love language, but remember, she can be aroused by other love languages as well. The more triggers you can leave around, the more your woman will want you when you're not there. Since expectation is such an important part of love, romance, and sex, your woman will be more willing and eager to please than ever before.

Building an Instant History

When you have a history together, she has another chance to think about you when you're not there and to fantasize about the two of you. When she remembers the experiences you've shared—your history together—she'll feel as if you've become a part of her life.

In the beginning of the relationship, you have no history together. How could you? You haven't had a chance, and you may be competing for a woman with someone else, someone with whom she already has a history. That's why you should begin building a loving-memory history together as soon as possible.

Your instant history is made up of the wonderful times the two of you have had together, making you feel close and a part of each other. The times you've loved, the times you've laughed, even the times you've cried together—these are the things that she will think about when you're not around. Good memories lay the foundation for the future of your relationship.

Building good memories into the beginning of your relationship has a double payoff. Not only do you get to enjoy good times together now, but someday, when things go wrong (and they always do), you'll have your good memories to draw on.

Don't wait for years of shared tastes and accidental incidents to accrue. Start creating your history right away. Even if you're not into music, pick a favorite singer you can share together and a favorite song that becomes "your" song. Do something with her that she's never done before, like hot-air ballooning, glider soaring, or scuba diving. When you're part of a first-time experience in her life, she'll remember you forever, like her first lover.

Take her to a live performance if you can. Make the night a memorable event. If you can afford it, do something extravagant first, such as renting a limo and taking her to a special dinner in an unusual location. You may wind up spending more than you would on a normal date, but the value is there if you're creating some instant history at the same time. She'll remember and cherish one exciting, different experience longer than many ordinary dinner-and-movie Saturday-night dates.

You don't even have to spend a lot. You can take her to an outdoor event, but in a very special way. When you pick her up, bring her flowers, a pillow for her to sit on, and a blanket to keep her warm. Pack a picnic basket, including her favorite food, a special bottle of wine, and, for later, a thermos of hot chocolate laced with crème de menthe or her favorite brandy. Always be sure to get her a souvenir program. If you're spending the night with her, plan something special for breakfast the next morning; don't just assume she'll make coffee and eggs.

Creating an instant history can be easy, even without money. All you need is a little imagination and you can figure out memorable but inexpensive things to do with the woman you love. Stage an especially erotic seduction centering around her favorite fantasy; include her favorite massage, aromatic scents, and music—and, of course, meaningful words from you. Throw a surprise potluck birthday party for her with all her friends.

Any special event in her life is an opportunity to build your instant history. For example, if she's moving, help her settle into her new place and then do something together, such as planting roses or fruit trees or putting up wallpaper, so that she always thinks of you when she enjoys the fruits of your joint labor.

If you're having trouble thinking of special events and surprises, think of the memorable things a woman may have done with you in the past. The day she made a gourmet picnic to take to the ballgame. The spring she planted the bulbs at your house that still bloom every year and make you think of her. The time she took you to the sex store to buy her a new vibrator. Or the day you bought the puppy together. Those are the kinds of moments that make up a couple's mutual history.

A client of mine is one of several mistresses of a very wealthy publishing mogul. "I'm number three," she quips gaily. "I don't try at all." But the truth is she does try, in a very clever way. She's the "staff photographer," documenting each of the mogul's special birthday parties, each gift, each new conquest he makes, selecting and keeping the photographic records. This allows her to wield a lot of power among the mistresses, since she gets to either display not-so-flattering pictures or destroy them, depending on her feelings toward the other women.

Since creating an instant history is so effective that it will work on almost anyone, make sure you've got the right woman before you try this technique. Hardly anyone can resist it, as I can personally attest. I had just met a man who I thought was okay, but he was no great thrill. As a matter of fact, he was quite fat, not at all handsome, and in the beginning I thought he looked silly when he looked at me with his in-love expression. Then he began to create an instant history.

Almost immediately, he invited me away for the weekend in San Francisco, where he was giving a lecture (a combination of instant history and "podium effect," explained below) and where I would meet other important people who thought he was wonderful. Soon after that, we flew to Catalina in a seaplane, landing in a spray of Pacific—all captured by him in photos presented to me afterward so that I could see how much fun we had had together. Then there was the trip to Big Sur, followed by more photos.

He happily courted my relatives and came to family parties, taking pictures and sending little albums to everyone afterward. Soon the whole family thought he was part of it, and we'd only been dating for a month!

Unfortunately, he was working without a Woman Plan. He had the right idea, just the wrong woman. I knew from the beginning he wasn't the man for me, but even I couldn't resist the instant history. Since instant history is so irresistible, always be sure you have the right man first.

As my own story illustrates, an easy way to reinforce your instant history is to document it with photographs. Every woman loves to have her picture taken. Taking her picture is a wonderful form of flattery. It shows that you think she's worth preserving.

If she has kids, make sure there are pictures of you and them together. A woman never throws out pictures of her children. When she sees you in photos with them, she'll become sentimentally attached by association. Also, be sure there are pictures of the two of you together.

As your relationship develops, put the photographs in a scrapbook for her to look at when you're not together. It's a memory jogger, to remind her of how important you are to her, of how much history you share. Think in terms of memories; they always trigger loving thoughts. We all think fondly of our past, even when it wasn't so great.

The Podium Effect

In order to have the in-love feeling, admiration for the love object is very important. We tend to love those we admire, so by getting a woman to admire you, you are paving the way for love. Since we all have a tendency to admire those whom others admire, one way to gain a woman's admiration is to show her how much other people love and admire you.

The podium effect is created whenever the woman you love sees you being admired by others. It's subtle and effective. She is swept away and charmed by the way other people look up to you and listen to you. She thinks to herself, "If all these people think he's so great, I'd better hang on to him. He must be a real prize."

No woman wants to be with a man other people think is a dork. She wants to be with a man she can be proud of. Although a woman may no longer aspire to be Mrs. Doctor or Mrs. Lawyer, she does want a man on her arm who makes a statement to others, a man who sends out a message that he is worthy of her love and admiration. Letting her see other people admire you is far, far better than telling her how wonderful you are yourself. Let others do it for you. She'll be forced to succumb to group pressure and admire you too.

When I was single, I found it awkward to explain to a new man I was dating that I was a respected author and lecturer, so I would invite him to watch me give a television interview or a lecture. Afterward, I could see almost immediately that the podium effect had worked. A man always admired me more after he'd seen me behind a podium or with TV cameras pointed at me.

Even if you're not on a television show or giving a lecture, you can create the podium effect. Invite the woman you love to a party where you've invited all of your closest and most loving friends. Let her see how much they admire you. Give their admiration a chance to rub off on her. Be sure to say something complimentary about her to your friends. Make sure your friends tell her how terrific you are. Let them know ahead of time that you'd appreciate it if they'd tell her only wonderful recent things about you, and no old war stories of the good old days.

Invite her to see you do anything you do well, whether it's hang gliding or playing chess. Let her admire your accomplishments. Just be careful not to bore her by over-exposure. Take her up in your glider, but don't make her airsick. Take her out on your boat, but not in a storm. Also, watch carefully to see if she's totally uninterested, in which case, do what you do well and don't push her to get too involved. Also, don't get so involved in what you're showing her that you wind up ignoring her completely and playing with your toy by yourself.

When you teach her a new skill, you gain podium effect just the way teachers do when they stand in front of a class. There are always students with a crush on the teacher simply because he or she is the expert standing in front of the room. Politicians do this all the time to gain votes.

To make the podium effect really powerful, combine it with triggers, anchoring, instant history, and repetition.

Repetition

Any successful love relationship has a necessarily habitual element. Books and love songs have been written about the addictive quality of love and how easily we become a habit with each other. If you know how habits are formed, you can easily become a habit with the woman you love— a habit that entails severe withdrawal should she wish to stop seeing you.

Repetition is one of the main ways habits are formed. Any act repeated in the same way over and over again becomes a habit, a minor addiction. Life's small rituals and the security we get from them can be very comforting, a source of solace when everything else falls apart.

You may think a woman wants something different and exciting all the time, but that's just not so. When it comes to choosing a man for the rest of her life, she wants someone who gives her a sense of security and permanence.

Once a woman has fallen in love with you, you can deepen that love and make her addicted to you. She can become addicted to your smell, the sound of your voice, the look on your face, the words you say, the affection you give, and especially the sex you two enjoy.

You don't have to be the greatest lover in the world. If you just know how to use the principles of addiction, she'll think you're the greatest. Begin with repetition, which will give her a sense of security and give you the appearance of being dependable and reliable.

Saturday Night—the Easiest Addiction

One of the most important things women want from a regular relationship is a date on Saturday night and on holidays. Not just one Saturday night but every Saturday night. Not just one holiday but every holiday. You can give her what she wants and get her habituated to you along with it.

Never underestimate the power of Saturday night. She knows it's your best night because you're not tired from work and you don't have to get up early the next morning. So if you deny her a Saturday night, she's going to assume that another woman got it.

Saturday night can definitely be the loneliest time of the week for a single woman. Next comes Sunday morning. But nothing's worse than being alone on Saturday night, unless it's being alone on New Year's Eve, when you can't even go home to your parents as you can on Easter, Thanksgiving, and Christmas. If you're not giving a woman holiday and Saturday night security, she's going to be downright unhappy with you, which is why women don't like to date married men.

After just a few regular Saturday night dates, she begins to expect to see you every week. And she looks forward to Sunday morning and the little rituals couples develop, such as reading the Sunday paper, going out for Sunday brunch, having breakfast in bed, or going jogging in the park. Soon she develops a habit of spending Saturday night and Sunday morning with you.

If business should take you out of town, or even if you're sick or have some other legitimate reason to miss a Saturday night, she'll find her habit interrupted. Suddenly, because you're not there and she expects you to be, she realizes how much you mean to her. She's used to your being there. She misses you twice as much as she would if you were seeing her only once in a while. She's become addicted to this time with you each week.

When you see her regularly on Saturday night, she begins to want Sunday and then Wednesday, and soon it's every night. She needs more of you. You, of course, will resist just a little so that she doesn't have "buyer's remorse" when you give in.

The repetition of your presence is a powerful force, and it works with anchors too. Repeat your sexual and good-feelings anchors whenever possible. The more you repeat them, the better they work.

Repetition doesn't enter the picture at the beginning of your relationship, but only when you're ready to make a commitment. As a matter of fact, you can judge the status of your relationship by noting the amount of progressive regularity involved. Does she want to see you two, three, or four times a week, even every night? Women seldom marry men they're not seeing constantly. The best relationships are those in which the commitment grows out of a steadily increasing regularity of time spent together.

"Our Song"

"Our song" combines well with repetition. The more often you hear it, the more it becomes yours. Couples in love often play the same meaningful music over and over again because for them it's a personal love-experience trigger, making them feel romantic and loving each time they hear it. The more they play it, the more they want it. "Our song" is part of the addictive experience that builds loving feelings.

You can add to your relationship by including any mutually shared love trigger that is habit-forming. You can have a song, a silly saying that has meaning only for the two of you, pet jokes that really aren't funny to anyone else, or private names for each other. These auditory triggers become a symbol of your love. Repeating them makes them more effective. For some couples, simply saying "I love you" becomes a self-perpetuating habit.

The Importance of the "L" Word

The "L" word (love, for those who have trouble saying it) is even more important than the "C" word (commitment) or the "M" word (marriage). You may get committed and you may get married, but if you're stingy with the "L" word, you're going to have trouble in your relationship.

Time and time again, couples come to me—some of whom have been together for ten years or more—with the woman complaining bitterly and feeling insecure because the man refuses to say the "L" word. If you can't say the "L" word easily, fluidly, and often (meaning at least once a day, more if necessary), you're going to have problems.

In order to have a good relationship, you must be willing to tell a woman that you love her as often as she needs to hear it. Saying "I love you" is a small sacrifice for domestic tranquility, peace, love, and happiness. If you can't say it for some reason, get help. See a therapist. Talk to your minister. Practice in the shower or while you drive to work in the morning. Say it over and over again until you say it easily and without hang-ups.

Saying "I love you" is good for you too. It helps dispell the demon doubts that plague anybody entering a relationship. By not saying it, you stop short of totally convincing yourself as well as the woman you want.

Don't think you can get away with saying something close. Only those exact words, "I love you," will do. Not "I'm here, aren't I?" Or "Sure, I do." Or "You know I'm crazy about you." Or "I'm yours, baby." Or "Does a bear shit in the woods?"

Nothing, not even "I care more for you than anyone else in the world," will take the place of "I love you." If you don't say the exact words, she'll never believe you love her no matter how many other ways you try to show her and tell her. You must say the words, or she will find someone who will.

To be extra sure, you might toss in a few of the magic words of her love language. If she's visual, you can say, "You can see how much I love you." If she's auditory, "You can hear how much I love you." And if she's a feelings woman, "You can feel how much I love you."

The Real Power of Praise

After "I love you," the next best thing you can say to a woman is something flattering. If you can't think of anything, say, "You're so beautiful." Or "I think you're wonderful." I don't know a woman who doesn't like to be told that she's beautiful. Women can't help it. We've been programmed from infancy to need approval for looking good. But we'll take any approval we can get.

If you have a choice between saying something critical and saying something that shows approval, and you want to have a nice evening, choose approval. Behind the approval statement is another statement that says you accept her faults and approve of her wonderful qualities, which obviously outshine her faults, which is why you're mentioning them and not the faults.

Truthfully, a woman likes the flattery, but what she really likes is the constant repetition of the warm, loving, good feelings she gets from being flattered. Those warm, loving feelings are addictive, and by flattering her, you become the giver of the good feelings, and she becomes addicted to you. Simple but very effective.

Flattery doesn't have to be fawning or sound dumb. Surely, with some loving thoughtfulness, it can come out easily and naturally. There must be something nice you can say about her. If not, why are you together?

For example, you're in her shower and you're using her soap. Later you could say, "That's wonderful soap you have in the shower. I like it better than mine. What kind is it?" Or "That's a clever way you've arranged this room. I'd never have thought of that." Or "I keep thinking about what you said yesterday" (and then quote her. Everyone loves it when you remember something he or she has said and when you indicate that it is meaningful to you). Then, if you really want to clinch it, you say, "I've been thinking how right you are about that." Everyone wants to be right. When you've had a disagreement, it's especially effective if you tell her later that she was right after all. That displays your flexibility.

Many women are concerned about making a romantic commitment because they're afraid of getting into a situation like their mother's, where the father was the boss and always got his way. Anything you can do to reassure her on this score—that you're not going to insist on having your way on every issue, that you will be flexible—will make it easier for her to commit to you.

On the whole, the way a woman becomes addicted to you, Mr. Right, is through the repetition of all the little pleasant habits and feelings she begins to associate with you over the course of your relationship. This gives her a feeling of stability and emotional security she doesn't find anywhere else in the world.

CHAPTER FIFTEEN

Handling Love's Problems

You've found the woman of your dreams and she seems to fit perfectly into your life. You're in love and she is too, and yet you're beginning to have problems. You're confronting the stresses and strains of becoming a couple, of melding two separate egos into a unit.

The problems range from "buyer's remorse," fear of loss, and jealousy to who gets which shelf in the medicine cabinet. Different couples have different problems, but almost every couple has some. Let's face it, falling in love is one thing; a serious, committed relationship is another. As the relationship gets serious, you're forced to face some serious issues. For many men, commitment itself is a problem.

"Buyer's Remorse"

Just six months ago, she was a vision, an unattainable fantasy. You could only dream about having her for your own—every day, every night. Now that she's said she loves you, you're thrilled, of course. But you're afraid it means an end to your "freedom."

LOSS OF FREEDOM

You're not exactly sure what you'd do with your freedom that you're not doing right now, but you hate to give it up. That's a normal reaction. All men have it. Some keep it in perspective; some let it come between them and a whole world of happiness.

For sheer crazy-making potential, loss of freedom ranks right up there with jealousy. I've had male clients who say, "I love her, but if I make this commitment to her, I'm giving up my freedom for the rest of my life." If you think of your freedom in the abstract, the idea of giving it up can become a big deal. So don't make yourself crazy; think about freedom in the here and now, in concrete, realistic ways.

Do you want the freedom to be alone again, and lonely? No, of course not. Okay, do you want the freedom to fuck whomever you want? (Because if you do, you're not going to keep your lady.) No? Really no? What specific freedoms do you want? To play poker with your buddies once in a while? To reserve Saturday afternoons for your softball league? Those are good things to bring up. Talk to her about them. She probably wants some time for herself too.

Succeeding in love means some inevitable changes in your personal lifestyle. If one of your important freedoms is the freedom to always remain the same, to never change or compromise, you will undoubtedly sabotage your relationship. If this is the case, you and I both know we're not really talking about freedom; we're talking about simple stubbornness. Life is about growing and changing. When you become part of a couple, you make a choice. You put your young playboy image behind you and move on to a new phase of your life.

ODIOUS COMPARISONS

Buyer's remorse can also set in when the conquest is over and you find out she's not perfect. You begin comparing your current woman with your mother or some woman in your past. Comparisons are very tricky, since every woman is so different and you can never find everything you want in one individual. So you start comparing Mary with Jane, who was a terrific skier. Mary falls down before she even gets her skis on, but she's a gourmet cook. Think fast—what's more important, fast skiing or fine dining? You see, comparing women is hard.

Better to compare how you have *felt* in each relationship. Are you generally happier, more content with your new love? If so, forget the comparisons. It's just another way of giving yourself buyer's-remorse craziness.

Unspoken Worries

When a romance becomes a relationship, there are always little frictions to smooth out, ground rules to be negotiated, and other concerns to be addressed. Until they are talked out, both parties will feel insecure. Yet many couples wait much too long to talk about these issues. They feel that bringing up anything serious or potentially negative will somehow destroy their romantic feelings.

WHAT SHE DOESN'T SAY

One way to improve communication and minimize insecurity during this transitional time is to listen for what she doesn't say. Avoid overreacting to vague words like "it, "that," "everything," "nothing," "they," "them," and "things." The danger is that the listener, you, fills in the particulars for a given vague word. Don't. Stop to ask what exactly she means and find out what the vague word actually refers to.

Let's say the love of your life has had a bad day. "Nothing's going right," she proclaims, and you, standing there listening, assume she's referring to your relationship as well as to everything else. Before you take her literally and assume you're part of the problem, ask, "Exactly what isn't going right? Tell me about it."

If she says to you, "I'm very upset," don't assume she's upset about you. Ask, "Exactly what are you upset about?"

What if she says, "Things are just not working out"? Now there's a statement fraught with dire implications. Don't let it throw you. Just say, "What isn't working?"

This strategy serves double duty. You find out exactly what's bothering her, and most likely it doesn't involve you. If it does involve you, you have a chance to speak up on your own behalf and to clear the air. Even if it doesn't involve you, you'll both have a nicer evening if she can say what's bothering her instead of carrying around unexpressed generalized hostility.

If the problem does involve you, don't avoid it or let her slur over it because you want to avoid trouble or the stress of working it out. Bring out problems as soon as you sense they exist. That way, you get to deal with specific issues before they actually do become generalized and infect your whole relationship.

MIRRORING HER IDEAS

Just when you think everything is going smoothly and you can see the two of you together for a long, long time, she comes up with some half-baked, weird-sounding scheme that makes you think one of you is nuts. "You know, I've always wanted to sell everything and buy an Airstream camper and travel around the country in it," she announces. Or "I've always thought I could be a great artist. I'm going to go to art school." Or "We could become beach bums for a year." Or something else that sounds equally off the wall, not at all what the woman of your dreams should be saying. That's when it's a good idea to mirror her ideas.

Mirroring her ideas isn't just a matter of repeating the words she's just said. It's a matter of checking out her intention and making sure you've understood what she really means. Mirroring her ideas will help keep you from jumping to conclusions. In any of the examples above, for instance, she could have been daydreaming about what retired life might be like for the two of you, and just blurted out her idea without giving it a time frame.

Susie and Jon came to me for counseling because they were having trouble communicating. Susie was always saying something that scared Jon or hurt him or gave him the impression that she didn't care for him as much as he had thought. Instead of telling Susie how he felt, Jon withdrew and sulked, which made Susie feel insecure.

When they came to see me, Jon had made up a list of Susie's indiscretions that went on for pages. He had written down incidents that went back three years, to the beginning of their relationship—times when she had said the wrong thing at the wrong time. It was the little things she'd say that seemed to break his heart and tear him apart. If she "wished we had a new car," Jon heard it as "I wish Jon made enough money to buy a new car." Then he felt guilty, then angry, then depressed, in that order, but he rarely told Susie.

When they were in my office, we went over Jon's list. He told Susie why each thing had hurt or upset him, and

she was genuinely surprised and sorry. "Oh, that wasn't
what I meant! Didn't you know? Why didn't you ask me?"
she wanted to know.

Susie's remark about going to art school was the one
that brought them to see me. Jon was distraught, figuring
Susie was trying to tell him that she was planning to run
off to Paris to art school, to live in a garret somewhere
with some unsavory artist type and never see him again.
Susie assured him it wasn't so.

Jon realized their communication problems came
partly from his insecurity about the relationship, and
Susie promised to be more sensitive to Jon's feelings. Most
important, Jon learned to mirror Susie by saying, "Are you
saying you'd be giving up your career and moving to Paris
to study and leaving me here?"

The simple technique of mirroring enabled Jon to deal
with Susie's frequent off-the-wall remarks and gave him
more control over the relationship. He began communicating more and not letting things fester for days and
weeks. After Jon stopped withdrawing and began speaking up about whatever was bothering him, Susie felt more
secure too.

Fear of Loss, and Jealousy

When you're in love and happier than you've ever been,
a part of you is also scared, because now there's more to
lose. You know that if this doesn't work out, you could be
hurt emotionally. You worry about investing too much
and then losing. You want to devote yourself to one wonderful relationship, you want to trust and believe, but you
have doubts that worry you. Once you start worrying, you
worry more, because doubts beget doubts.

You're suffering from fear of loss.

You're afraid of losing the love you're just beginning to enjoy. Having a good relationship seems too good to be true, especially if you've had bad experiences with women before.

If you have trouble believing you deserve a happy, loving relationship with a woman who adores you, failing in a relationship can be a self-fulfilling prophecy. That's why it's important to remember that some fear of loss is normal, but fear of loss shouldn't dominate your thoughts about the relationship.

Some men torment themselves worrying that they're "not good enough for her." Remind yourself that you are unique and have wonderful qualities. No matter what you think is wrong with you, women have loved worse. They have loved outlaws and abusers, deviants and downright bastards, macho morons and lazy bums. Surely you deserve love too.

If something in your past you absolutely can't erase is keeping you from enjoying the present relationship, see a therapist as soon as possible. Shop around. Ask your friends which therapists they've seen who've helped them. Clear up your problems from the past so that you can enjoy the present.

Even if you're not plagued with self-doubts, you should be aware that some fear of loss almost inevitably comes with the in-love feeling. Some fear of loss is normal, but it can make you act in ways that are detrimental to your relationship.

Psychologically speaking, everyone wants to control the source of his or her pleasure, so you have a built-in desire to control the woman you love. You can't totally control her, so you become stressed and vaguely insecure about the relationship. Even a normally confident guy can find himself being unreasonably jealous of other men when fear of loss comes up.

OTHER MEN

It's almost impossible to meet a woman who hasn't been involved with other men at one time or another. Any woman you meet is sure to have had other men in her life who may still be around. There's her yoga teacher, her boss, her tennis pro. There's the man she dated or was married to just before she met you. And the one before him and before him, all the way back to her high school sweetheart, who still calls her every once in a while.

Just thinking about all those other men can make you nervous. They're like vultures waiting to pounce, or at least that's how it looks from your vantage point.

The same addictive quality that makes us closer and leads to commitment in relationships can be the source of jealousy. After all, the more you're addicted to the woman you love, the more you fear losing her, the more you feel a need to control her. Jealousy is fear of loss at its worst.

Nobody is immune from jealousy. I've comforted countless weeping women whose loved ones were drifting away with some "bimbo." (The other woman is always a "bimbo," just as the other man is always a "jerk.") I've seen men ruin perfectly good relationships because they thought the woman they loved was "doing it" with someone else. I've even had attacks of jealousy myself.

In the 1960s, we really believed we could have it all. Commitment and freedom to explore other relationships, security and love, spontaneity and truth. Actually, jealousy was always there, even in the experimental "free love" communities, and it was always painful. It just wasn't acknowledged.

Now, because of disease, sex with the wrong person can carry a terrible price. Monogamy is not just a moral or lifestyle choice; one partner's infidelity can be life-threatening to both. Jealousy now involves more than wounded pride, and it is more emotion-laden than ever.

YOUR JEALOUSY

The green-eyed monster comes in two versions: jealousy and envy. Jealousy means you wish she would stop doing something she's doing, such as seeing someone else or just spending too much time on activities that don't involve the two of you. Envy means you wish you were doing whatever she's doing too. Envy occurs when you wish you could dance as well as she does. Jealousy occurs when she goes out with a good dancer and you're worried about losing her to him.

Jealousy hits you in your gut in exactly the same place you feel attached to the woman you love. It attacks suddenly, when she mentions having heard from an old love that day, or when she breaks a date, or when a man's business card with a number scribbled on it falls out of her purse, or when she just seems less than thrilled with the idea of the two of you being together. You'll never believe she's doing her hair or some other lame excuse. You know deep in your heart that she's with someone else, and it kills you.

You become jealous when you doubt your own ability to hold on to your loved one—when you doubt yourself. That's when you're most susceptible, when you're ready to suspect a lie or an infidelity.

Women expect a man who really cares to show some jealousy. Just how jealous to be, however, is a fine line for a man to walk. If you let her think you're crazy-jealous, she may decide you *are* crazy and dump you for being so much bother. If you don't act jealous at all, she may dump you because she thinks you don't care enough.

"But what if I'm not the jealous type?" No jealousy at all is just asking for trouble. The woman in your life will never believe you care enough, and you may find her leaving you for someone who she assumes cares more. Act a little jealous; it's good for your relationship. Besides, you should be a little jealous.

"But what if my jealousy is eating me up? What if I can't control it? What if I want to kill her and whomever she's with when it's not me? What if I want her to be with me all the time and never look at another man at all?" Well, that, too, is destructive to a relationship. It's nice for your lady to feel loved and to know how much you care, but enough is enough. No woman wants a man who's always angry and jealous and suspicious.

Out-of-control jealousy changes your personality from loving to demanding, from reasonable to paranoid. You call her at odd hours to check up and see if she's really where she said she'd be. You imagine she does strange and wonderful sex acts with other men. You wonder if she moans louder for them when she comes. You wonder if you'd escape prison if you killed her lover in a jealous rage. You feel tacky, stupid, and angry at both yourself and her.

WHY WE GET JEALOUS

According to Freud, jealousy instilled by loss of mother is inevitable. Freud said, "Jealousy is one of those affective states like grief, that may be described as normal. If anyone appears to be without it, the inference is justified that it has undergone severe repression and consequently plays all the greater part in his unconscious mental life."

So if either of you finds a little jealousy creeping into your life from time to time, you're just having a normal human reaction.

FIRST AID FOR JEALOUSY

1. Don't simply withdraw from the relationship on circumstantial evidence.

2. Admit your jealousy. Being jealous is nothing to be ashamed of, especially if you have an understanding about exclusivity. Fooling around is no laughing matter. Speak up; tell the woman you love that you feel angry, hurt, and/or jealous. Never be accusatory, just say how you feel.

3. Don't shout or throw a tantrum, but don't mince words either. Tell her you feel jealous, not that you feel "uncomfortable."

4. Find out for sure if there's any reason for you to be jealous. Ask her, calmly, reasonably, "Should I be jealous?" And if she says, "No," try to believe her.

5. Never, ever, under any circumstances, give way to the urge to ask about the other man, even if you find out there is someone else. Never ask, "Is he richer than me?" Or "Is he better in bed? What did you do with him? Where did you go?"

6. Never confront the other man to get rid of him. It may work once with some men if you're especially big and tough, but eventually she'll fool around with someone bigger and tougher, so it won't work forever.

7. Ask, but don't demand. If your own insecurities are placing unreasonable demands for fidelity on a woman before she's ready to love only you, you could drive her away. Sexual fidelity comes from mutual agreement, not on demand.

8. Strong self-esteem is the best defense against jealousy. You have to really believe you're so terrific she'd be a fool to want to be with anybody else. Besides, you wouldn't want someone that nobody else wants, so of course there are going to be other men who've found this wonderful woman besides you. But of course, she'll want only you because you're so special and you have so many special things to offer, and she's a smart enough cookie to realize

that. Should you hear about someone else in her life, someone richer, more powerful, more handsome, don't let it worry you. After all, if she's with you instead of him, you must really be terrific.

9. Jealousy is all about losing someone. By remembering that you can't really own another person, you'll have less fear of losing that person.

10. Jealousy can have a reverse effect. It can cause you to want a woman who isn't at all right for you. You may hardly be interested until you find out she's dating someone else, and then your interest is sparked. Suddenly you can't live without her, and you're even more jealous.

11. Sometimes jealousy is justified. If there are constant clues of infidelity, if you feel paranoia every time you're apart, it may be that your partner really is cheating on you. If so, get it out in the open fast. Don't let her get away with sneaking. Find out what's going on. Stop her affair, firmly and without hysterics, before a casual fling becomes a real love affair.

12. If she is involved with someone else and won't stop, totally and immediately, don't stay in the relationship. If you let her get away with being unfaithful while still having the ongoing pleasure of your company, you invite her to break your heart, to step all over you and treat you like dirt. You are saying to her, "I don't care how much you abuse me, I still love you." If you find yourself in this position and can't get out of it, get help from a therapist immediately.

HER JEALOUSY

You want the woman you love to be just a little possessive, maybe just a tad jealous. How much is okay? If you feel flattered by her jealousy but can readily reassure her that it's misplaced, that much is fine.

When her jealousy becomes a problem and you can't seem to convince her of your fidelity, then you have a woman who is out of control. She's not reasonable. She's dangerous. She ruins every outing by being jealous. She says and does terrible things and accuses you of infidelities you hadn't even thought about.

Inevitably, the women who come to me with problems of jealousy are fixated on their jealousy. They can't control their jealousy or think of anything else. Sometimes, though, there are extenuating circumstances.

Evelyn and Stanley came to me because she was so chronically jealous that they were having trouble being together. It seemed that Stanley had this thing for big-breasted women. Evelyn had even offered to have plastic surgery, but Stanley said that wouldn't do. He couldn't control his fantasy, and every time he saw a big-busted woman on the street, he watched her until she was out of sight. This, of course, made Evelyn very upset.

To make matters worse, Stanley had had an affair with a big-busted women two years earlier and confessed it to Evelyn. That gave substance to, and fed the fires of, her suspicions. She was always watching and waiting for him to run off with another big-busted woman. Although they had been together almost twelve years, Evelyn was terminally insecure about their relationship.

Stanley tried to reassure Evelyn by telling her, "I'm here, aren't I? I've been here for almost twelve years. I'm not going anywhere. There's nothing wrong with guys liking big tits. There're even magazines about big jugs just for men like me. I've shown them to you. Can't you see I just want to look. I'm not leaving." His reassurances weren't good enough.

For Evelyn, just knowing that there was some other kind of woman that Stanley would rather be with made her constantly operate out of fear of loss. Stanley, on his part, had grown to like Evelyn's constant groveling and begging. Knowing how much Evelyn feared losing him made Stanley feel superior and powerful, so his reassurances were always rather halfhearted, and interspersed with longing looks at big busts.

Evelyn and Stanley had fallen into a pattern of jealousy and hostility. Breaking that pattern wasn't easy. Evelyn had to learn to replace her insecure, jealous thoughts with positive ones. She also had to stop feeding Stanley's need for power by reacting every time a big-busted woman came near the two of them. When Stanley saw that he didn't get a rise out of Evelyn anymore, his interest in big breasts became less of a driving force in both their lives.

Reassuring a jealous woman doesn't work, because when you say, "Oh come on, you don't have to worry," she hears, "You have to worry." If you say, "I'm faithful, you know I am," she thinks, "How do I know?" The more you try to reassure her that she shouldn't be jealous, the more she thinks about how jealous she is. The longer you are mired in talking about whether she should or shouldn't be jealous, the longer her jealousy will continue. Trying to talk her out of being jealous, or coddle her out of it, or romance her out of it, will only make it worse.

If you're involved with a jealous woman, forget trying to keep her jealousy under control. It's impossible, and the harder you try, the worse the jealousy will get. You know it's her low self-esteem that makes her insecure and jealous, so you try to build up her self-esteem. That doesn't work either. Her low self-esteem and the causes of her jealousy may have started long before she met you, and she may need years of therapy to get over those problems. Nothing you say will cure them.

Realize she's just a jealous person. Realize, too, that jealousy is normal and that some people are more jealous than others. Accept that you are getting some wonderful benefits from the relationship that keep you involved. If you want the benefits to continue, you will have to learn to deal with her jealousy. Here are some rules.

DEALING WITH HER JEALOUSY

1. Don't lie. She'll sense you're lying and get really upset. Admit you looked at or thought about someone, but add, "No big deal." And don't make a big deal about it. Don't start a fight, declaiming your innocence. Fighting over jealousy only makes it more important.
2. Don't treat her with extra loving kindness when she's jealous. She'll only learn to act jealous to get love.
3. Don't put down her feelings. Talk about them with respect, but assure her you don't like her actions.
4. Calmly reassure her that you love her and don't want anybody else.
5. If reassuring her of your fidelity doesn't help, get her to a therapist. She needs counseling, not promises of fidelity.

PREVENTING JEALOUSY—BUILDING TRUST

It doesn't matter whether jealousy is rational or irrational, the pain still feels just as bad. The person who is jealous suffers much more than the other person in the relationship. The jealous person is taunted day and night and suffers whether there really is something to be jealous about or not. Only absolute truth between people will prevent jealousy.

When you tell each other the truth over a period of time, trust and unassailable credibility are the results. When a woman catches you in one small lie, the distrust is likely to carry over into other areas.

MONOGAMY

If you're involved in a relationship you think has a real future, have a very serious and frank talk about truth, exclusivity, and jealousy. Tell her how you feel about dating other women and how you feel about her dating other men. You may both decide you're ready to give up all others, or you may arrive at some understanding, or ground rules, about how monogamous you will be. With the advent of sexual diseases that may kill, the issue of monogamy can come up as quickly as the issue of sex.

Here are some suggested ground rules.

1. Until you both agree to be monogamous, you will practice safe sex only; or
2. You will refrain from all sex until you enter a committed, monogamous, relationship, at which time you will both be tested for sexually transmitted diseases before becoming sexually active with each other.
3. Once in a monogamous relationship, you will undergo further testing after a conservative interval before engaging in anything other than safe sex.
4. You will both agree to immediate full disclosure should you fall prey to sexual indiscretion. If that happens, you will agree to go back to ground rule #3.
5. If you want to do something that isn't covered in the ground rules and that might provoke jealousy (for example, you want to invite an ex-girlfriend out to lunch just to maintain the friendship), talk about it *first,* not afterward.
6. Make honesty and trust your first goal in establishing a good relationship.

CHAPTER SIXTEEN

Don't Fight

Any relationship, no matter how good, has conflicts from time to time. Achieving a good relationship involves some testing. You both need to know how the relationship bears up under problems. The trick is to resolve those problems without fighting.

Since men and women fight so differently, there is practically no way you can come off looking good when you fight with a woman. Because you are bigger and louder than she is and because she cries, you're going to wind up looking like a bully whether you win or lose. Sure, you can overpower her vocally, or even physically, but she'll resent it and eventually find a way to get even with you.

Even when a life-and-death, make-it-or-break-it relationship issue is involved, and there seems to be no other way to solve the problem, avoid fighting. Fighting adds anger and resentment to an already difficult situation. When you fight, you risk having her mad at you because you yelled at her and bullied her, not to mention whatever she was angry about in the first place. Fighting to solve an argument is counterproductive.

This does not mean that you can't have a lively discussion. We all know the difference between a discussion and a fight. A fight is when she cries and you yell, when you both storm around, stamp your feet, and bang on things with your jaws set and the veins standing out on the sides of your necks. An argument can be tony, upscale, literate, even fun (as in a Noël Coward play). A fight is tacky and degrading.

If you're like most men, a constant diet of scenes and fighting is enough to sour you on a relationship. And why not? We used to think that fighting cleared the air, that the best thing to do with your anger was to release it. Now, new studies show that expressed anger often creates more anger.

We've all known couples for whom fighting seems to be a way of life, but they don't seem particularly happy and they're definitely no fun to be around. For them, fighting clears the air and makes them feel better when they make up. But a real-life *Who's Afraid of Virginia Woolf?* is a rotten way to live.

And men aren't the only ones turned off by constant bickering; women are too. So she's going to want to know how you go about resolving differences. Are you going to bully and shout and demand your own way all the time? Is she going to live a life of constant battles? Are you reasonable or unreasonable? Can you live without getting your way?

If you fight with her over every issue, she's going to think, "I'm not going to spend the rest of my life fighting with this man. I'm going to get him out of my life and find someone nicer." She may concede a point just to shut you up or get the battle over with, but she'll remember giving in and she won't like it.

When you fight, you create negative anchors for the

person you love. She begins to associate you with unpleas-
ant scenes, berating and name-calling, shouting and bully-
ing, instead of loving and caring.

Even if you're right in the point you're making and you
win the battle at hand, your woman will remember every
nasty remark you made in anger. The fight may be over,
but the memory lingers on, tainting your relationship and
staining your love.

Women Who Need to Fight

Some women try to get you to react, to be jealous, to fight,
to be angry. If a woman is always baiting you, trying desperately for a reaction, it's because she's not getting
enough love and attention from you. Like a difficult child,
she needs to make you angry with her so she can be
convinced you care.

If you find yourself in a relationship with a woman who
needs to fight, try giving her more love and attention
rather than giving in to your desire to outfight her or
ignore her. If, however, you're involved with a woman
who needs physical violence as assurance that you care,
get her to a therapist as soon as possible before she goads
you into behavior you'll regret.

When to Give In, When to Stand Firm

Just because you're not going into battle doesn't mean you
have to give in all the time and let her have her way. The
division of power in a relationship is very delicate. Although you may believe you should be in charge at least
half of the time, that's not how life works out. In real life,

each of you will be lucky if you get your way even one quarter of the time, and both of you will compromise the rest of the time.

So how do you know when you're making too many compromises or when you're letting her have her way too often? You can tell because your self-esteem falls to a low ebb and you start to feel bad about yourself. You begin to resent her for making you change more than you want to, and you begin to dislike yourself for letting her walk all over you.

How to Stop Fighting

There are approaches that lie between fighting all the time and always giving in, ways to get what you want in your love relationship without doing battle.

The reason we're so easily sucked into fighting with our loved ones is because the issues are often charged with the secret message "If we can't work this out, then it's all over."

Rule number one in any disagreement is to defuse the issue. Reassure the woman in your life that just because you can't agree doesn't mean the relationship is in danger. What it does mean is that you're going to deal with the problem calmly, reasonably, and without hurting what's most important, your love for each other. It may mean that you'll wind up simply agreeing to disagree on that one issue.

To break out of a fighting cycle and into a loving one, call "time out" and remind each other of a time when you were happy together.

Beth and Jerry had been dating for two years when they came to see me. By then, they were caught up in a real *Virginia Woolf* screaming and fighting cycle. They had almost forgotten how much they had once loved each other. By taking them back to the beginning of their relationship, I was able to find a time when Beth and Jerry were really happy together. It was when they were camping alone together in the High Sierras.

As Jerry and Beth remembered how happy they were during that camping trip, I had them recall what it was they loved about each other. Their faces softened as they remembered that loving time. Then they touched, anchoring the happy feelings. Jerry found that this technique could calm Beth down and get her in tune with him, which at least was a start toward ending the fight.

After a few sessions, Jerry and Beth had a whole arsenal of alternatives when it looked as if they were headed for a fight.

Reflecting

Reflecting, a special way of verbally mirroring your loved one's behavior, allows her to slow down and look at things from your point of view. Use reflecting to get into agreement with the woman in your life.

For example, she complains that you haven't been taking her out enough or spending enough time with her. Instead of arguing over who's right and who's wrong, or trying to defend yourself by giving her examples of all the time you have spent with her, first try reflecting what she's really saying. Let her know you understand.

If she's visual, say, "It looks as if you feel unloved because I haven't been giving you enough attention lately." If she's auditory, say, "It sounds as if you feel unloved because I'm not spending enough time with you." Or if she's a feelings woman, say, "I sense that you feel unloved because I haven't been spending enough time with you."

Once you're in tune with her feelings (not necessarily meaning that you think her anger is justified or that she's right, just that you understand why she's upset), then she'll be better able to listen to you. You'll be agreeing instead of disagreeing.

Reflecting your loved one's feelings, even in the midst of an argument, can bring you close again. Suddenly, instead of disagreeing, you're on the same side. Since it's really hard to keep fighting with someone who's agreeing with with you, the battle can be over as soon as you want.

Venting

When things just don't seem to be going right, when evenings together end in disappointment, when she starts a fight over something that's not important, when you sense that something's bothering her and she's not talking about it, then venting can work miracles.

Venting means that instead of simply reflecting her complaints, you solicit them. Rather than saying "I can see why you're angry" and letting it go at that, you add, "And what else is bothering you?" Or "Is there anything else that I do that you don't like?"

Lots of women are afraid to start arguments with men, so they never say anything about what's bothering them unless it's the most outrageous complaint, such as "You shouldn't have slept with my best friend, you son of a bitch." Otherwise, a woman feels her lesser complaints are too trivial, not important enough to risk a fight with you. The trouble is, the small problems add up and become big problems. Venting helps get them out in the open. When they are not secret anymore, they lose importance.

She may never say that anything's bothering her, but she can still be carrying around a mental check list of complaints she's been collecting about you. Then, one day, she blurts out, "I've had enough! I just can't take it anymore!" and you're stunned, wondering what the hell is wrong with her. The way to avoid sudden, unexplained explosions is to clear the air every once in a while. Venting is perfect for clearing the air.

By allowing your lover to get rid of the long (or even short) list of grievances she's carrying around about you, you can get your relationship back to the loving place you want it to be—but first you have to let her vent.

The trick is to stay calm and not take her complaints personally. This is not the time to debate each one or to point out the fallacy in her thinking. As a matter of fact, if you do that, you will cut off the lines of communication, and she'll stop telling you what's wrong because she doesn't want to start an argument.

For example, the woman in your life complains that you're not spending enough time with her. She says she doesn't come first with you. You know she does, but instead of arguing and putting her down for being so needy, you say, "Maybe I haven't been spending enough time with you. Why don't we find ways of spending more time together?" Then you ask, "Is there anything else that's bothering you? I sense that you're still upset."

What if she says, "You don't call me often enough" or "You don't make dates far enough ahead" or "You don't say 'I love you' often enough"? The trick here is not to deny anything, but to give her the feeling that you're taking each of her complaints seriously and will try to do something about them.

In one brief venting session you can find out exactly what's bothering her. Once she gets started, you'll be amazed how the rest comes rolling out. The advantage to you is that you will get a full list of every real or imagined grievance that could have been affecting your relationship for weeks, months, or even years.

Even though you may feel unjustly accused, just listen

and reflect her complaints back to her. She'll feel better for just having said everything that's been bothering her, and she'll be in a much more conciliatory mood. She'll be relieved, and by your listening and letting her know that you can find some area of agreement, she'll be even more convinced of how much you understand her.

After she's run out of complaints, go back over her list and deal with every problem area. Find out exactly how big a problem each one is for her. Once she's released all that pent-up anger, you'll be surprised to find that the steam has gone out of most of her complaints. If some of them are potentially serious relationship problems—she wants five children and you hate kids—at least you'll have them out in the open.

If you find that there are serious problems to deal with in your relationship, one or more of the following techniques can smooth the way.

Self-Disclosure

Self-disclosure is a new way to get close and to solve arguments. Self-disclosure means you reveal something about yourself that's similar to her revelation. You disclose having had similar feelings and so she trusts you more.

Charles was in love with a woman who didn't like his dog, Blue. Blue had been his buddy for seven years. Charles had raised Blue from a pup and had let him sleep in his bedroom. Alice, Charles's fiancée, who had grown up on a farm, said Blue was just a dog and belonged out in the yard and not in the bedroom. And Blue wasn't just in the bedroom. He was on the sofa and eating off the kitchen counters; and whenever Alice stayed overnight, Blue stole her clothes and tore them to shreds.

Charles would yell at Blue but his heart wasn't in it. He

always felt, "Love me, love my dog." He and Alice were always fighting over Blue, and soon Alice was refusing to be anywhere near the dog.

Finally, Charles began agreeing with Alice. "Actually," he finally admitted, "I've realized for a long time that Blue is out of control [a self-disclosure that put him in agreement with Alice]. I've been worried about what he might do next. It's getting expensive having him tear up things all the time. I've been thinking about getting a dog trainer to work with him." Which is what Alice wanted in the first place. Once she knew they were on the same side about Blue, she began to actually like the dog.

Winning With Humor

Humor is one of the best ways to defuse any argument. One reason we get so angry with one another is because we forget to "keep it light." You can often make the same point with humor and achieve a better outcome than you would by fighting.

David and Penny had been dating for two years when they came to see me. David was an engineer and a manager of a large manufacturing company. Penny, a textile artist, worked at home. David was very neat. Penny was more than artistically disorganized. David refused to go to Penny's apartment anymore, but even that didn't help. "There's no place to sit down at her place," he complained, "and if she comes to my place, it's a mess in two minutes. I can follow her trail everywhere. She just drops her clothes and stuff all over the place."

Penny was beginning to feel badgered and annoyed with David. "I want to be able to relax," she said, "and not have to be worried about what David's going to think all the time. If I want to leave my work out when I'm doing something, I should be able to do that. I don't mind how he keeps his things, and he should mind his own business about my stuff."

Although David and Penny seemed to be very much in love with each other, their disagreements were starting to take up more of their time together. Soon they were almost always bickering about Penny's mess.

Amazingly, when David learned to lighten up and joke about Penny's messiness, she became neater. He learned to use humor to get what he wanted without fighting. Instead of accusing her by saying, "This place is a mess. Why don't you ever put anything away?" he learned to use humor. "I guess I caught you in the middle of spring cleaning again," he would quip. Or he would say, "I'll just sit here on top of this pile of papers."

When David brought up Penny's mess, she immediately began feeling guilty and started preparing for a battle. "I'm sorry. I should have cleaned it up."

But instead of starting their regular fight, David kept it light: "Oh, no problem. I'm getting used to it. It's sort of like a new decorating style. Don't worry about it."

Penny was totally thrown off by David's change of pace. Since part of her behavior was just a way to defy David and show him that she could be as messy as she wanted, being messy lost a lot of its appeal. She began to clean up, not totally, not forever, not perfectly, but the improvement was noticeable.

David and Penny began to get closer and to talk to each other about much more intimate subjects than ever before. By removing their regular fight over Penny's mess from their relationship, they were able to appreciate the really important qualities each of them had.

Often an issue simply disappears when one person says it's no longer important.

The Broken Record

In spite of your best efforts, a battle breaks out. You can't stop yourself, you can't stop her. What do you do? If you continue fighting, you're going to escalate what probably started out as something minor into something major. The broken-record technique is one of the best ways to fight without escalating the battle.

In the broken-record technique, you acknowledge the other person's right to have an opinion different from yours, and you also reaffirm your right to maintain your own opinion. For example, Howard, a client of mine, was battling over what he believed was an important issue with Carol, the woman he loved. Howard's hobby was flying, but after an especially rough flight, Carol had decided she never wanted to fly in a small airplane again. Howard loved flying and felt he was a very safe pilot. Every time Howard and Carol planned a trip together, they wound up in the airplane battle.

Carol would say that she wished he would never fly in a small plane again. Whenever he did, she just worried about it crashing until she knew he was safe on the ground again. She claimed he was risking his life, and she didn't want to risk hers as well.

"I'm a good pilot," he would shout. "I have six hundred hours in the air, and flying a small plane is safer than driving on the freeway."

"I don't care," she'd yell back. "You're just going to get yourself killed. I feel a lot safer flying in a commercial plane with bathrooms and stewardesses and air-conditioning. Besides, small planes cost too much."

Neither of them was willing to give in on the issue. It seemed as if their life together would continue to be one long airplane battle—until Howard learned how to use the broken-record technique whenever Carol brought up the subject.

"I hate it. It's dangerous," she'd shout. "And if you really loved me, you wouldn't fly."

"I understand how you feel, but it's important for me to continue to fly," Howard would answer evenly, first getting into agreement with her feelings, then simply restating his opinion without getting angry.

As Howard calmly repeated his stand, Carol got even angrier at first, but then she simply ran out of steam. No matter what Carol said, Howard refused to argue. Without raising his voice or getting excited, he simply agreed with her and then restated his position.

Soon Howard felt better about his relationship because he wasn't getting angry and upset anymore. Carol gave up because she realized that Howard wasn't going to fight with her and that he wasn't going to change his mind either. She soon began to accept the airplane, although she remained adamant about not liking it. When adults get together, they have to accept the fact that they are not always going to like everything the other person likes, nor do they have to.

Compromise

Most of these techniques for avoiding knock-down, drag-out fights are not so much sneaky ways for you to win your point, as they are effective ways to reach a mutually agreeable compromise (or a respectful "agreement to disagree"). Any mature relationship involves constant compromise.

Your own willingness to compromise is an indication of how important you feel the relationship is. If you wonder whether you're in love or not, examine your willingness to compromise. The more willing you are, the more in love you are.

CHAPTER SEVENTEEN

Casting a Spell

"My ex-wife's getting married." Patrick, a thirty-nine-year-old insurance adjuster, was visibly upset because the woman he'd been married to four years before was remarrying. He had just been to a Christmas party where the happy couple announced their engagement.

"I hated to see how she adored that guy. She never acted that way around me. All she did was hang on him and laugh at every dumb joke he made and brag about how wonderful he is. It was absolutely disgusting.

"And then he acts like she's so sexy. Making remarks about what a wild woman she is. She was never that sexy when we were together. I tried to be pleasant, but it was eating me up inside. I guess I didn't really want her to be happy without me.

"But, of course, she didn't care about my feelings at all. She hardly noticed I was alive. She acted drugged or dazed or something. She seemed hypnotized by this guy into some kind of altered state of consciousness.

"After I went home, I couldn't get the look on her face out of my mind. She never looked at me like that. As a matter of fact, no woman ever has.

"I don't understand it. I'm not that bad-looking, I'm nice to women, I try to be sensitive, but women just don't get crazy about me, like my ex is about him. How does he do it?"

Easy.

The Magic of Love

When you're in love, you seem to float through life on a cloudlike cushion of air, and the world is a wonderful place. Colors are brighter, music sounds more beautiful, and every love song seems to be sung just for you. You are blinded by your feelings; you are indeed in an altered state of consciousness.

What is it that makes a woman fall madly, totally, unbearably in love, so that she feels as if she needs to be with a man all the time? She may say, "He makes me feel happy" or "I feel complete with him" or "He makes me feel beautiful."

When she's with the man she loves, the feelings go beyond close communication to some almost extrasensory experience. The fact that she can't pinpoint exactly what he does to make her feel so wonderful is often written off as the "magic of love" or as "chemistry."

The man she loves has thrown a mysterious psychic net over her, and she can't escape. She is under his spell. She is his love slave, willing to do almost anything to be with him and to keep him happy. He's her prince charming, her white knight, her yuppie superman, intelligent yet intuitive, forceful yet sensitive.

How does a man put a woman under such a spell?

What's the secret? The secret is that some men intuitively know how to speak a woman's love language in a special way—by telling stories that cast a magic spell.

Now, you can learn to cast the same powerful spell. You'll learn exactly what stories to tell and exactly how to tell them. You'll have the added advantage of understanding exactly why the story induces a state of trust and relaxation, of acceptance and agreement, in the woman you love.

By telling simple little stories, by stating your case in certain words to the woman you love, in a certain sequence, you can get her to agree with you, to make changes in herself or your relationship, and to like making these changes. You are about to learn how to get exactly what you want from the woman you love.

Setting the Stage

Plan on taking her out to dinner. If you cook, plan a special dinner for her at home. When a man provides a woman with food, it's symbolic of his desire and ability to provide for her. Feeding a woman and sharing a meal also have sensuous overtones. The smell of good things cooking, the act of being fed—they give us all a feeling of love and comfort. From childhood we've loved the person who feeds us, beginning with our mother. Giving food is one of the best ways to establish a warm and agreeable atmosphere.

Dress comfortably. If possible, mirror what she'll wear. Let her know ahead of time: "Why don't you wear warm-ups tonight. We'll be casual. That's what I'm going to wear." Give her a chance to get in tune with you. People who are dressed alike feel more comfortable with each other. Wear her favorite after-shave—surely you know what that is by now! If not, find out first. Spray her favorite scent around or burn her favorite incense.

If you have a fireplace and the weather's cool, light a fire. Burn nice-smelling wood, another ritual that appeals to a primal sense of comfort and increases her trust in you as a provider. You want to make her feel as relaxed and receptive as possible. So when she arrives, make sure your place will be almost womblike in its warmth, good feelings, and safety. Plan ahead so that the flow of the evening isn't interrupted.

The Right Music

In order to have her in the most receptive mood, choose a piece that approximates sixty beats per minute—the most relaxing tempo because it simulates the human heartbeat, induces trust, relaxation, and receptivity.

Superlearning experts who have researched how this state is best achieved suggest the slow movements of the baroque composers—Bach, Handel, Vivaldi, Corelli, Telemann, and Pachelbel. Some easy-to-find choices are Vivaldi's *Four Seasons,* Handel's *Water Music,* Corelli's Concerti Grossi nos. 3, 5, 8, and 9, and Pachelbel's Cannon in D. Or, in a more contemporary vein, try the new-age music of Steven Halpern, Georgia Kelly, Paul Horn, or George Winston.

Don't arouse her suspicious by making too many unfamiliar romantic gestures. When men do new and extraordinary things, women begin to wonder what's going on. Hopefully, though, you've been romantic before in your relationship—with flowers, candlelight dinners, music, and elegant wine—so that all of these recommended niceties won't put her in a state of shock.

Tonight, when you're finally ready to cast your spell,

you'll simply combine the romantic gestures you've used separately before, orchestrating the evening into a seductive heaven where she's open to your every suggestion.

Getting Her to Say Yes

When you're talking to the woman you love over dinner, be attentive—and be sure to bring up enough loving memory triggers and anchors to assure that the romantic mood continues. Remind her of the wonderful vacation you had together or the great New Year's Eve.

After dinner, relax together. Look at some photos of a recent event you both attended where you had a wonderful time. Get close to her so that you can touch her and be able to watch her at the same time.

Before you begin casting your spell, make sure she's fully relaxed. You can tell if the tension lines ease near the corners of her mouth or eyes. Notice her breathing. Is it rhythmic and even?

When you're sure she's fully relaxed and receptive, invoke one of your good feelings anchors as you talk. At the same time, sit the way she's sitting and breath the way she's breathing. Begin to time your speech to the pattern of her breathing, breaking your phrases and taking a breath when she does.

The Spell-Casting Formula

Spell-casting is done with four simple statements. The first three are obviously true—statements with which you know she will be in immediate and comfortable agreement. The fourth statement is not necessarily true, but you want her to agree with it anyway. And she will.

Modulate your voice and talk slowly. Think of yourself as a modern-day Svengali casting a hypnotic spell over some unsuspecting young woman. Make the statements in a low, soothing tone, pausing briefly after each one and giving her time to verify and accept its truthfulness by checking it against her own experience.

The first two true statements will be phrased in her love language. For the third true statement, you will shift to another love language, and for the fourth (not necessarily true) statement, you will come back to hers.

One important reason she will believe and accept the fourth (not necessarily true) statement is because her subconscious yearns to return to her own love language. By changing the love language in the third statement to one that's different from hers, you make her subliminally uncomfortable, longing to get back to the peak of comfort that you've so skillfully created. She'll agree to anything because the comfort state is so pleasing to her.

Here's an example of how casting a spell works. Let's say you want her to make a real commitment—to agree to a life together and to agree to set a wedding date. You're tired of fooling around and playing the dating game. So far, she's been reluctant to agree to definite plans for your future together.

You touch her good feelings anchor and say, "Seeing how beautiful you look tonight [the first statement in her visual love language], watching that great log burn in the fireplace [the second statement in her visual love language], listening to the fire crackle [the third statement, but not in her love language], you can picture the two of us together until we're old" (the fourth statement, returning to her visual love language). The last statement isn't necessarily true, but she's going to agree because the spell-casting has mesmerized her.

Casting a spell is deceptively simple. On a superficial

level, you appear to be making simple observations about the two of you and your evening together. On a deeper level, you have constructed a very carefully framed series of statements that make her psychologically want to agree with you.

Your first three observations are so unarguably true—and mostly pleasant—that she is seduced into going along with the last observation. Your mirroring and anchoring earlier in the evening have put her in the mood. Your first two observations in her love language now crystallize her mood into one of willing agreement.

Your third observation is equally true, but in another love language. Subconsciously she is momentarily disoriented and becomes anxious for you to return to her more comfortable love language. When you do return to it in your fourth statement, she automatically embraces what you say. Although she never consciously notices the shift in language, her subconscious registers it and reacts.

Casting a spell is not unethical, unless you do it for unethical reasons. The above example certainly isn't unethical, because you know and love the woman and sincerely desire a lasting relationship, and because you're not trying to induce her to do something illegal or contrary to her deep moral beliefs. You can get what you want from her by casting a spell, partly because you know the psychological techniques and partly because what you want is probably pretty close to what she wants, only she doesn't know it yet.

In many ways you are mirroring her unspoken, perhaps as yet unacknowledged, feelings. A part of her wants what you want, and when you cast a spell, you bring that part to the surface. The safer a woman feels with you, the more secure your relationship is, and the more she'll let you lead her by casting spells.

When you prepare to cast a spell, figure out exactly what you're going to say and practice ahead of time.

There are all kinds of spells you can cast—spells for love, spells for sex, spells to turn her on.

Seductive Stories

Seductive stories are spells that motivate your loved one, not only to agree with you but also to take action. To do something you want her to do. Suppose you want her to be more aggressive sexually. You want her to make the moves, and no matter how much you hint, she doesn't seem to react. When you actually say something to her about being more aggressive, she gets defensive and angry and withdraws. Tell her a seductive story and convince her easily.

Always start your seductive story in her love language. If she's visual, start out visual. Say "I can picture us alone together on a beautiful tropical island. We're lazily watching the sun's reflections in the languid lagoon." Then switch to feelings. "Then I rub you all over with suntan oil till your nipples and clit are all erect." Finally, back to visual: "When you see my erection, you jump on me and slide right down on it."

If she's auditory, you could start by saying, "Last night I listened to the sound of your breathing when you slept, and I could hear the rustle of your body against the sheet when you turned. I looked over at you and thought about the wild, exciting sounds you make when you come."

If she's a feelings woman, you could start by saying, "Even when you're not here, I sense you next to me. I can feel your body touching mine. I hear your voice, breathing, and then I feel you taking my cock in your mouth." Or whatever language you feel comfortable with.

Seductive stories can induce her to action. You can also use spell-casting to solve problems in your relationship.

Little Spells to Solve Problems

When casting a spell to solve a problem, you simply talk about the problem while using spell-casting techniques.

For example, you want to have a big family as soon as possible. She wants to continue her career and postpone childbearing. She's afraid of falling off the career fast track and not being able to get back on. Instead of arguing with her and driving a wedge between the two of you on this very important issue, agree with her objections.

If she's visual, you say, "I can see where having children right away could disrupt your career." (The first agreement in her visual love language.) "You look as if you're on the fast track, and I can picture you going right to the top." (The second agreement in her love language.) "It sounds to me as if you don't want to have children until you're a little more secure in your career." (A third agreement, but in an auditory and feeling love language.) "The way you look tonight, though, I could just picture you with a little baby who looks just like you." (A fourth observation, and not one she necessarily agrees with, but she will feel drawn to agree because you have cast a spell.)

You have mirrored her objections with two agreements in her visual love language, then you have thrown her off balance with an agreement in auditory/feelings words, finishing with an observation in her visual love language. She will automatically be drawn to agree with the last statement because she agrees with the first three statements and also because she wants to return to her comfort-zone love language.

Or, if you have an auditory woman, you might say, "I hear what you're saying about not having children right now. It sounds to me as if you think having a baby now would sound the death knell to your career." (Two agreements in her love language.) "I understand how you feel about motherhood." (A third agreement, but in a feelings love language.) "But I say you'd fall right in tune with motherhood. I can hear you singing lullabies already." (A fourth observation, in her love language, which she's drawn to agree with.)

For a feelings woman, you might say, "I sense that you feel having children now would upset your career plans. I understand how hard it would be for you to be torn between your career and a child." (Two agreements in her feelings love language.) "It looks to me as if you can't see yourself having children for some time." (Another agreement, but in a visual love language.) "I just feel that you'd be such a loving mother." (A fourth observation, in her love language, which she's drawn to agree with.)

With practice, you'll be able to think of three agreements to make before you bring up what you want. It's best to plan it all out ahead of time, because each new situation will need its own script. But you need to spend only a minute or two thinking about what you're going to say.

On the spur of the moment, try conjuring up little spells to fill different needs. For example, you've just been invited to a class reunion. Your auditory woman overhears the conversation, and you can hear the lack of enthusiasm in her voice. She doesn't want to go with you, but you want her to go.

You say, "I can hear in your voice that my class reunion sounds like a big bore to you. You don't want to listen to a bunch of strangers talk about the good old days." (Two auditory agreements.) "You're afraid you might get trapped into looking at old yearbook graduation pictures." (A third agreement, in feelings and visual love languages.) "But there would be some interesting people there to talk to, and afterward we could go to a special place I've always wanted to take you—a quiet country inn by a babbling brook." (The fourth statement, in her auditory love language, is not just convincing; it's also a subtle negotiation, pointing out the benefits to her.)

When you start out agreeing with a woman, she really listens to you. If you start out disagreeing, a part of her turns off and goes into a defensive mode. She's so busy thinking about how she's going to defend herself that part of her stops listening to you. When a woman hears that her position is being validated by you, her unconscious feelings of resistance fade and are replaced by a desire to be agreeable.

Secret Messages

Secret messages—or "imbedded commands," as some people call them—are a way to get your woman to do what you want without actually asking her. A secret message can be indicated by emphasis or a change in your tone of voice. Your secret message can be imbedded in a statement that sounds like the opposite of what you want.

An older but still randy gentleman I know had an interesting secret message. He would approach a young girl and say, "You wouldn't want to go out with an old man like me." He intuitively knew that people often don't hear the negative messages, or if they do, they usually ignore them. With his special change in tone, the young girls would hear the secret message, "You want to go out with an old man like me," even though that wasn't what he said.

Perhaps you've noticed how your woman sometimes forgets exactly what you told her not to forget. "Don't forget to return the video tape," you tell her on your way out the door. And of course she forgets because her conscious mind has missed the "don't" part of your message, and all she has heard that really registered was "Forget to return the video tape."

The principle is the same as if someone said to you, "Don't think about pink elephants." Your conscious mind finds it hard *not* to think about pink elephants. In communication, all forms of "don't do" are unreliable. If I said to you, "Don't think about airplanes," some type of airplane or some recollection of travel on an airplane would probably be the first thing that jumped into your mind.

Since the positive message dominates, change your negatives to positives. Instead of saying, "Don't forget to return the tape," say, "Remember to return the tape." Instead of saying, "Don't forget to pick up the cleaning," say, "Be sure to pick up the cleaning." If you get in the habit of using positive rather than negative requests all the time, your message will be more effective. You'll be able to communicate better with the woman you love.

Advertisers understand the reverse advantage of using negative messages. When they say, "Don't shop here first," they know you'll hear, "Shop here first." When they say, "Don't buy our brand before you've tried the others," they know you'll hear, "Buy our brand before you've tried the others."

Secret messages are useful in lots of situations. For example, you're ready for a committed relationship and she says she's committed to you, but she sees more of her ex-husband than you like. You don't want to tell her not to see him at all, but you'd like her to cool it. You say (to your visual woman), "I can see why you don't want to lose Jack's friendship. I sense how fond you are of him, and I can see why you don't want to stop seeing him."

The secret message is "You want to stop seeing him."

Imbedded Questions

Another kind of secret message is the imbedded question. Instead of asking her something outright that might put her on the defensive, you make a statement. For instance, you're curious about her ex-husband. Instead of saying,

"How come your last marriage broke up?" you'd be better off using a secret question hidden in a statement. "I can't imagine *why your last marriage broke up*" won't put her on the defensive.

Or, for example, you're spending the night at her place and you want to know if she has food in the house for breakfast (because she usually doesn't). Since her empty fridge is a sore spot you've argued about before, this is a good time to use an imbedded question. Instead of asking, "Is there any food in the house that isn't rotten?" say, "We haven't discussed what *we're going to cook for breakfast.*" That way you're making a statement and giving her a chance to participate in the decision rather than putting her on the defensive. Not only that, but you have an imbedded message: "We're going to cook breakfast."

Parables

A parable is a story you tell to persuade a woman to change her mind without getting into an argument with her.

A client of mine was becoming very serious with a woman who worked for a big corporation that always sent her on long trips to the Far East with male colleagues. He was bothered and a little nervous about her spending so much time away from him, but was smart enough not to demand that she give up her job or any part of it. He felt he was really ready for marriage. She, on the other hand, wasn't ready to commit. Her objection was that he'd been married three times before. She wasn't ready to be number four.

Instead of demanding that she marry him right away, he used a clever parable to get her thinking about settling down with him in spite of her objections. He would ask her, "If you were going to take a long airplane trip, say around the world, and you had your choice of going on a new sleek airplane that looked beautiful but had never been tested or flown before, or going on a reliable plane like a 747 with some trips behind it, which would you feel safest on?" Before long, she got the message, without any arguing. He had made his point loud and clear, and she couldn't help but be impressed.

When you have to talk to her about something, think about the outcome before you just burst out with what you want. Don't argue, demand, or whine. Instead, tell her a little story filled with secret messages. You'll get what you want and have peace on the home front as well.

Weaving It All Together

If you practice the technique of telling seductive stories and parables with hidden messages, it will come easier to you. Soon you'll feel natural casting a little spell over your woman. It will be fun for you and captivating for her.

The little spells you cast will merge into an ongoing romantic web she'll willingly step into whenever she's with you. When she's away from you, she'll yearn to be with you again because you speak her language. She wants to do whatever makes you happy because you've asked in such a subtle way.

At first, you may worry that she'll resent your reading her mind and knowing her inner thoughts, seductively leading her to do things she may not have done before. Don't worry, though. Have you ever seen a woman in love who didn't look deliriously happy?

You're her prince charming, the one who provides the magic of love. You can make her want to be with you forever.

CHAPTER EIGHTEEN

When Love Happens

At last you're in love and so is she. You know you're in love because you think about her obsessively all the time. You can't wait until you see her or hear from her or touch her again. You can't concentrate on business, and you don't care. She's more important than your job, your friends, or your family. If she's depressed or unresponsive, you fret about it and worry whether she's falling out of love with you. If she's happy, you're happy. You realize you have to marry her just to get your life back on an even keel.

You picture the two of you together forever. You start to think about having children with her. You begin to worry about the future in a way you never did before. You worry about getting ahead, making more money, and buying a house. You imagine your wedding and you think about how you'll ask her. You worry about whether you can afford a big enough ring.

When you're not with her, you spend most of your time telling anyone who will listen how wonderful she is. You know she's the most beautiful, the most intelligent, the sexiest, the kindest, simply the greatest woman that ever existed.

If she has a quality that someone else might see as negative, you see it as cute and admirable. If she's stubborn, you see it as stick-to-itiveness. If she's messy, you see it as her artistic personality. If she cries easily, you see it as sensitivity.

You know you're in love because your friends are starting to look bored when you launch into another of your conversations peppered with cute and clever things she's done and said. Your friends do comment, however, on how much happier you seem and how good you look. Of course, you're watching your weight, going to the gym, running around a lot with love's endless energy, but you're not accomplishing much except being in love.

You know you're in love because all other women, even the new cute ones that you see, pale next to the woman you love. Only she wears the magic halo your love bestows. At last you see why all the other women you've ever known were wrong for you. You've found your one true love, the one you were meant to be with forever.

You know you're in love because you're committed to working out the problems that come up from time to time. You're willing to go through the testing period that couples normally have before they learn to trust each other totally.

Clinching the Commitment

If you've followed the Man Power Method exactly, avoiding such mistakes as giving too much too soon, letting her learn to treat you badly, or being too romantic too soon, you won't have any disappointments when it comes to making her yours forever. She'll want to be.

You should, of course, have noticed increasing signs of commitment along the way. If you've missed too many of them, you may be rushing into a committed relationship too soon.

The Steps to Commitment

You begin dating every weekend.
You assume you will spend holidays together.
You begin seeing each other all weekend and during the week as well.
You have a regular schedule for being together.
You are happy with your relationship 90 percent of the time.
You miss each other whenever you're apart.
You give each other little gifts.
You take vacations together.
You sleep together almost every night.
You meet her family and she meets yours.
You propose, or she does, or you start living together.
You discuss having or not having children.
You acquire property together (house, car, television, VCR), which is assumed to be community property.
You begin to commingle monies in some way.
You decide to marry and make lifelong commitments to each other.

Asking the Big Question

You and she have become a committed couple, going everywhere together, and you think it's time the two of you moved in together. You know she's in love with you, but you want to make sure she's ready before you ask. What do you do?

Set the stage the way you would to cast a spell. Use love triggers and memory anchors to get her into a receptive mood. Get in tune with her. Mirror her. Talk to her in her love language. Breathe in rhythm with her.

Then, when you've followed her for a few minutes, shift into a new position. You could sit up straighter, lean forward, cross or uncross your legs. See if she follows your move. If she does, then you know the time is right to ask. If not, start over until she's following your physical lead.

Next, start to lead her to the commitment you want. Get her to agree with you verbally and physically. For example, you've mirrored her and now she's mirroring you. Since you've both been sitting back, you now lean forward and say, "If we lived closer together, it sure would be easier. We wouldn't have to be carrying our stuff across town all the time."

She leans forward and says, "This constant commuting is killing me too. Whatever I need is somewhere else." She's not just agreeing, she's following you physically, so you know she's not feeling pressed and that she's very comfortable with the direction the conversation is taking.

You lean back and say, "We should try to find a way to spend more time together with less commuting."

She leans back and says, "I agree. We'd have more time to actually be together that way."

She's still following, so you know it's safe to pop the question. "Okay, so why don't we look for a place together, halfway between my job and yours. We'd save lots of time and probably money too."

She agrees that the two of you should start looking, but you know it's not a halfhearted agreement or one that she has doubts about. You've led her, step by step, to commitment.

If at any point she had stopped following you or offered a different point of view on the problem, such as "Maybe I could leave a few things at work," you should immediately back off. This means she's not ready. Never push a woman into a commitment before she's ready. Always test before you ask. There's no excuse for creating a deadly awkward moment or being put down. You should always know ahead of time when a woman is ready to say yes.

Overcoming Resistance

She's encouraged you all along, and now, when you're ready for a greater commitment, she seems to be pulling away. You know she loves you and yet she's holding back. She's potentially capable of making a commitment, so how do you find out what's wrong and overcome her resistance?

By being supportive and gentle, you can find out what's wrong. Don't argue or demand. Don't get upset. If she senses that you're upset, she may just pull further away instead of confiding in you.

To the visual woman say, "It appears that you have concerns, and I want to look at the problem with you. What do you see that makes the future appear so cloudy for us?"

If she's auditory, say, "It sounds as if everything isn't as harmonious with us as I thought, and I want to be totally in tune with you. Tell me what you're thinking."

If she a feelings woman, say, "I sense that something's troubling you about us. You know your feelings are safe with me, so relax and share them with me."

No matter what the problem is, you must find out about it to deal with it successfully. As long as she doesn't tell you, whatever's bothering her will become more and more important.

When you do know her objection, you can turn it into

an asset. For instance, she says she can't marry you now because her career is just begining to take off and she can't take time away to get married. You say that's good, because then you can elope.

She says she can't marry you now because neither of you has any money. You say if she marries you, you'll be inspired to make more money.

She says she's not ready to settle down and have children right now. You say she can get married now and have children later.

By airing a problem, you get a chance to contribute your perspective about it. You may find that the problem can easily be solved, or that it's not a problem after all. Or she may change her mind and marry you in spite of the problem. At the very least, once the problem is out in the open, it loses the power of being a mysterious, unknown obstacle.

Advice From Friends

It's almost impossible to avoid getting advice from friends. They all think they're experts in romance and that they know what's best for you. The trouble is that their advice is colored by their experience, not yours.

Even if your friends are wise enough not to volunteer advice, you may be tempted to ask. Even if you don't ask them directly, you'll be telling them all about her. Unfortunately, every cute little quirk that delights you may not live up to your buddy's fantasy of what a woman in love should be like. So he says, "Hey man, I wouldn't put up with that. She's out of line. You're not serious about this girl, are you?"

Or you confide to your buddy, "I've never felt like this in my life. She's so incredibly beautiful, and she's so hot

I can't believe I'm so lucky. She can't get enough of me."

"I worry about that kind," he says. "They've been around too much. Besides, I don't like it when a woman's pushy. First she wants sex, sex, sex, then it's money, money, money. Those types always want more. Besides, if she's that hot with you, she's been that way with other guys too. Doesn't that bother you?"

Suddenly you're not so happy as you once were. The bloom is off the rose, and you begin to wonder whether you're really in love and whether she's really in love.

Never listen to your buddy when he tells you what he'd put up with and what he wouldn't. You don't know what he'd really put up with if he had the chance. Probably things you'd never imagine.

Don't Screw It Up

Naturally, you have moments of doubt and insecurity, worries about what the future holds for the two of you. If you do have these moments, if you're taunted by little voices asking, "Are you sure you're doing the right thing?" simply tell the little voices to shut up. Most important, keep your fears and doubts to yourself. She probably has some of her own, and hearing about yours isn't going to make her feel any better.

Go for the gusto when it comes to love. You know what drives a woman away—criticism and coldness. You know what keeps a woman coming back—love, affection, and emotional security. The choice is yours. Shower a woman with real understanding, acceptance, and appreciation, and she'll never leave you.

Keeping Love Alive.

When you've found the love you want, keep using the
Man Power Method. If you watch the signals your woman
gives you, you'll be able to read her mind forever. You'll
always be able to keep her happy because you can stay in
sync with her inner self.

Start your discussions with agreements. Speak to her in
her love language. Anchor her love to you. Use the Man
Power Method techniques to resolve problems and avoid
fights. Pay attention to her. Mirror her for conscious harmony and keep casting your love spells around her.

By continually using the Man Power Method, your
woman will always want to be with you. There isn't a
woman alive who can resist a man with the knowledge
and skills you have. You know the magic. You can create
the chemistry of love. It will be with you alone that she
finds love and security. She will be yours forever.